·Cycle·

CENTRAL AMERICA

A FRAMEWORK OF ROUTES FOR
EXPLORING SOUTHERN MEXICO,
GUATEMALA, BELIZE AND HONDURAS

Researched and written by
Ian Benford

MAPS

This guide is designed to be used with recommended, separately bought maps of the area.

There are two companies which produce good quality maps for this region. **ITMB** and the **Rough guides**. Their maps can be bought in most good travel bookshops and over the internet at **www.itmb.com** and **www.roughguides.com**.

The following ITMB maps are recommended, and referred to in this guide. However, they have do have some errors and omissions. These are noted at relevant places in the text.

- The Yucatan Peninsula, 1:500 000, 2005 edition (waterproof paper and index) – also includes Belize, and northern parts of Guatemala. This map doesn't include San Cristobal de las Casas, Chiapas, although a map on pg 41 covers this. (Older editions cover all of Chiapas and include plans to Cancun and several ruins)
- Guatemala, 1:470 000, 2005 edition (waterproof paper and index) – including parts of Belize and northern Honduras. Contains useful street plans of Antigua and Guatemala City. (Older editions have some useful plans of ruins)
- Honduras, 1:750 000 – including much of El Salvador and northern Nicaragua. Contains a street plan of Tegucigalpa.
- Belize, 1:350 000 – includes small parts of neighbouring countries.

The whole region can be covered by buying the first three maps.

ITMB also produce a map of all Central America, which is useful as an overview, but the scale is too small for navigation.

Rough Guides in association with the World Mapping Project have produced two maps:
- The Yucatan Peninsula, 1:650 000 (waterproof paper and index)
- Guatemala/Belize 1:500 000(waterproof paper and index)

ISBN 1-905006-00-4

Acknowledgements
Richard Andrews of Pedalpower and Mayapedal
Helen Brose
Michael Shawcross
Thanks to Ben,
John and Annette Seekings
and John Potter

Disclaimer
This guide was researched during five extended visits over a period of seven years. The author has tried to ensure the accuracy of the information, but cannot accept responsibility for any loss, injury or inconvenience incurred by users of this guide.

CONTENTS

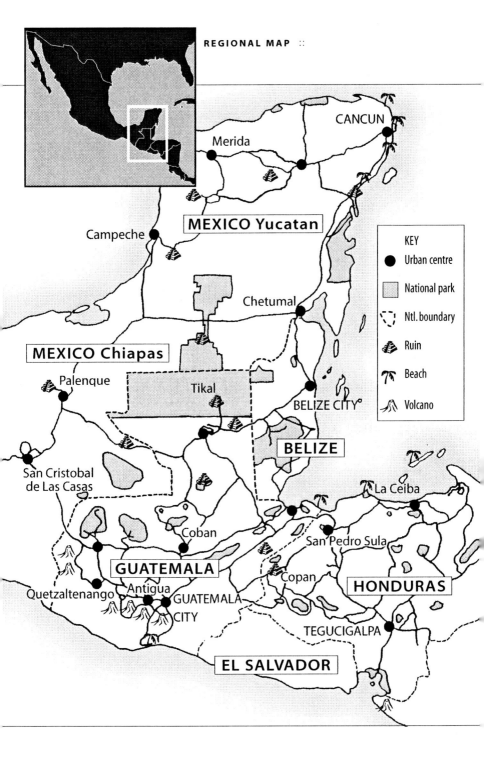

CANCUN

Merida

Campeche

MEXICO Yucatan

Chetumal

MEXICO Chiapas

Palenque

Tikal

BELIZE CITY°

San Cristobal
de Las Casas

BELIZE

La Ceiba

Coban

San Pedro Sula

GUATEMALA

Copan

HONDURAS

Quetzaltenango

Antigua

GUATEMALA
CITY

TEGUCIGALPA

EL SALVADOR

KEY

● Urban centre

National park

Ntl. boundary

Ruin

Beach

Volcano

Introduction

This region is the home of Mayan peoples, who have a fascinating culture and beautiful ruins. The Latins have added colonial splendour, with elaborate churches, squares and cobbled streets.

There are an incredibly diverse range of landscapes, including thick jungle, cloud forest, semi-desert, volcanoes and pristine palm shaded coastlines. Because the distances between areas of interest are usually less than 50 miles (80km), the region is perfect for cycling.

A framework of routes on paved and dirt roads has been researched for touring, with off-road trips and other excursions suggested around cultural or beautiful locations. The coverage is extensive, and one of the aims was to find interesting ways of getting from A-B, so there are often a choice of routes, depending on interests, fitness and time.

The guide is not just for cycle purists, alternative transport possibilities are suggested for the few monotonous sections or where the climbs are particularly long and hard.

There are many advantages to touring on a bike, including:
- Being able to go where you like, when you like and being able to stop at leisure.
- Enjoying the journey between places, not just snatched views from a bus.
- Getting around towns and cities quickly and for free.
- Meeting local people who are not tourist hardened.

The draw backs are few:
- Occasional bus and boat rides can be bit more expensive.
- Learning to trust people to look after your locked bike, whilst visiting ruins, churches or markets is not always easy.

The reality is, with the information given, a good map, and a bicycle of choice, it's possible for anyone to have a good time and take an incredible experience home with them.

Going there (and getting home)

Flying
Flights direct to capital cities are usually more expensive, but it's easier to arrange longer stays this way. Charter flights to holiday destinations like Cancun are relatively cheap, but inflexible, usually only for 1 or 2 weeks. Although it's worth trying for longer stays, they do come up occasionally. Buying a return ticket to and from different places is much easier these days E.g Flying to Cancun in Mexico, and out of San Jose in Costa Rica.

The internet seems to be the easiest place to book one destination return tickets, for tickets involving flying in and out of different destinations a travel agent will be of more help.
NB Last minute bargains seem to be harder to find, with nearly all airlines now increasing fares in the last week before departure.

To the Yucatan, Mexico
Cancun is the main airport in the region. There are direct flights from many airports in North America and from Britain, The Netherlands, Belgium, Spain and Germany in Europe.
Merida also on the Yucatan peninsular, takes flights from some N. American destinations.
To Belize – Belize city has the only international airport.
To Guatemala – Guatemala city has the only truly international airport, although Flores in Peten has one or two connections to neighbouring countries.
To Honduras – Tegucigalpa, San Pedro Sula are the two main international airports, and the island of Roatan has started to take charter flights from abroad.
NB There are significant departure and airport taxes when flying out, check whether they have been included in the flight cost.

Internal flights
There are several companies servicing the region, although flights do tend to be very expensive for the distances covered, and it's normal to have to pay extra for carrying a bike.

Overland
Most choose the Pacific route down through Oaxaca in Mexico, because the coastal scenery is so beautiful and the roads are relatively quiet, not to mention the beaches, surfing etc. The section from Salina Cruz to Tuxtla Gutierrez is not so interesting and the road starts to get much busier after joining the highway.

Alternatively there is good cycling around Oaxaca City, to the local ruins of Monte Alban, and some serious off-roading in the mountains north of the city. The road south toward the Pacific coast drops spectacularly through deep valleys. Once again though it's probably worth taking a bus from nearer the coast to Tuxtla Gutierrez or San Cristobal.

By sea
Apparently there's a scheduled seasonal boat from Tampa in Florida to Progresso in the Northern Yucatan.

Going home
It can be very expensive buying a ticket locally for a flight back from Central America, the exception is Cancun, where some of the charter airlines offer cheap one-way fares to Europe and North America. There are many travel agencies and it's a good idea to get a couple of quotes before buying.

Flights usually need to be booked at least 10 days before travelling in order to get the best

value, so chilling out on the Caribbean coast or cycling across the Yucatan peninsular for a few days, are two options whilst waiting.

When to go

There are only two seasons in this region, wet and dry. The dry season usually starts in December and ends in May, although this can vary by a couple of weeks or so with on going climate changes. It gets significantly hotter from February onwards until the rains start to break in April, and this is important to bear in mind especially if wanting to cycle on the coasts where it can be blisteringly hot. Also some areas can start to appear quite barren towards the end of the dry season, which can make December/January a good time to start a trip, in order to catch areas at their verdant best.

The wet (now marketed as 'green'!) season can be a good time to travel, there are fewer tourists, although unpaved roads can quickly become difficult after rain, and there are more mosquitoes.

The winds generally come from the south east, although there can be northerly winds in December and January which will normally bring in mixed weather, and sometimes rain.

Topography defines the temperatures which can vary from 35°C (95F) and hotter on the Pacific plains to less than 10°C (34F) in rain lashed mountains, and there can be frosts at very high altitudes. Normally, however, in the highlands, temperatures during the dry season are pleasantly between 20°C (68F) and 30°C (85F), although it's still worth avoiding the midday sun.

Local variations – The Honduran Caribbean coast has an extra dry season in August and September, although it can rain at any time. In the mountainous regions there is always the occasional possibility of rain, or more likely low cloud and mist, it's just less likely during the dry season.

Hurricanes – which arise in the wet season, can be devastating, southern Honduras and northern Nicaragua took a long time to recover from Mitch in 1999. There will normally be a build up, and a few days warning of an approaching storm. The aftermath can be extremely chaotic for several weeks; although a bike is often the best way to avoid the inevitable landslides and rock falls on the roads.

Money

Travelling with a mix of cards, travellers cheques and cash covers all eventualities.

US dollar traveller cheques are the safest way to carry money. Although they may be difficult to cash in rural towns. Keep a separate note of the numbers and receipts

Cards are readily accepted in most towns throughout the region. If carrying more than one, try to keep them separate, as a back up. Make a separate note of expiry dates, card numbers, and the cancellation procedures.

NB Doing over the counter transactions, with a passport and card for cash, is becoming increasingly difficult as the banks now rely on cash machines.

US dollars are used everywhere, and easy to exchange for local currency, although try to make sure it's carried in small denomination notes, accidentally pulling out a $100 bill can be embarrassing, and getting change can be harder, unless at a bank. Torn notes are often refused.

Banks in some form are available in anything called a town in the text, although in the smaller branches, card transactions may be difficult, or they may only have business relations with only one of the major card companies, which can add a transfer charge. There are often long queues, and it can be time consuming to do across the counter card transactions.

Many banks are now opening on Saturday mornings, but not all.

If the banks are closed, it's possible to ask to pay for someone else's groceries at a supermarket or fuel from a garage with your card, before getting them to give you the equivalent cash. (this will obviously need some Spanish, as it can get confusing).

Western union and other money transfer outlets are available everywhere, and easy to use. You will need a transfer number to pick up the money, easily sent by e-mail from the person sending the funds. The charges for transferring money vary, but are normally about 15%.

Costs

These will depend very much on where you plan to spend most time. In the mountains and countryside away from tourist areas it can be hard to spend more than US$15 a day.

Basic budget costs per day, not including excursions or entrance fees.

	Tourist hotspots and large towns	Countryside
Mexico	$25	$18
Guatemala	**$20**	**$14**
Belize	$30	$20
Honduras	**$18**	**$13**
Nicaragua	$17	$12

It is easy to live on less, the compromises come with less eating out, drinking less beer and other manufactured drinks and camping more.

NB Prices of private tourist trips like launch rides and tours have increased considerably over the last five years, whilst the prices of ruins and museums have risen more steadily.

Safety and Insurance

- The best insurance against theft is common sense. For example, it's a bit daft taking an very expensive bike to a country where the average rural wage is less than US$5 day.
- Keep travellers cheques, cards and passport under clothing in a moneybelt, and photocopies of these documents somewhere else.
- Consult your governments official internet travel advice for latest information on safety, and possible changing entry requirements for the countries to be visited. Also find out and take a note of the addresses and telephone numbers of your national embassies or consulates in these countries, if it all goes wrong, they will be the people you need to contact.
- Travel and medical insurance should be comprehensive i.e covering all medical bills and repatriation (with your bike) in an emergency. Not all standard policies will cover cycle touring and any other adventure activities planned, so check the small print.

Fitness and health

Before travelling

- Ideally to cover most of the distances between places, the ability to cycle about 50 miles (80 km) a day on mixed terrain and enjoy it, is fine for most of the routes described. Some of the climbs are long, but the gradients are usually reasonable.
- There are several serious diseases to avoid in Central America, check with your medical professionals which vaccinations and other preventative measures will be needed, two months before travelling.
- Check if your prescribed medication is legal in Central America, and take a copy of the prescription with you.

- If going for longer than a few weeks getting your teeth checked over is a good idea.

Whilst travelling
When cycling it's important to keep your body happy, eat before being hungry and drink before getting thirsty. Little and often sums it up.

If do you get ill, give yourself time to recover, beyond simply feeling better, to let your body get it's strength back. This helps reduce lingering symptoms and possible re-occurrence of the problem.

The list below is not supposed to be exhaustive, but covers the common health problems likely to be encountered:

Sunburn – skin protection has increasingly become an issue when travelling to a hot climate. Gradually increase your time of exposure to the sun over a few days. Shoulders, fore arms and faces suffer most, a peaked hat and a light, long sleeved shirt will prevent the worst. Sun blocks and high factor lotions are important for sensitive skins. Try to start cycling early, and avoid exposure in the midday hours. Having a siesta is a good habit to get in to.

Ticks – wearing trousers when walking through vegetation will lessen the chances of having to deal with them. If travelling alone, a small mirror is useful to check awkward areas of your body. Sharp nails or tweezers are good for the 'twist and pull' from as close to your skin as possible.

Dehydration – when cycling in a hot climate it's possible to need to drink several litres of water over the day. Keeping your urine pale is a good rough guide to staying well hydrated.

Mosquitoes – covering up is the best protection, at night a net and spray will stop nearly all of these little nasties, and save sleepless nights. For anti-malarial advice ask your doctor.

Altitude Sickness – caused by reduced oxygen levels at higher altitudes. Give yourself time to get used to altitudes over 3000m, avoid over exertion and have plenty of rest breaks.

Diarrhoea – unpleasant at the best of times, it is unfortunately, very common. Keep drinking water(add some salt to aid rehydration) and avoid food, if starving, dry (non sugary) salad biscuits seem harmless. If yourdiarrhoea involves blood, seek medical advice.

Sand flies – are smaller than mosquito's, and will require a finer mesh for protection, however they are only common on certain beaches and therefore avoidable.

If any unusual symptoms persist beyond a couple of days, then it's always worth seeking professional medical advice.
A range of pharmaceutical medications are available from most towns. For minor illness, if you can explain your symptoms confidently, medicines can be sold over the counter.

A basic first aid kit should include;
Plasters, bandage, and elasticised tubular bandages for knee sprains and general support.
Iodine, as an emergency water purifier, and for sterilising wounds.
Rehydration salts, antiseptic cream and suncream/block.
Surgical tape for holding nasty cuts together until proper medical treatment.
Insect repellent, although a good quality net will work for nights.

Herbal medicine
This complementary healing is making a come back in Central America as it is in other parts of the world. There are plenty of local herbalists and suppliers throughout the region, although many of the local products sold will be unfamiliar.

A couple good examples that are in wide use are:

Apazote (herb from markets)	Good for stomach infections
Manteca de cacao (pastel from pharmacies)	Excellent for damaged skin. e.g sunburn

The following list of well known products have all proved useful:

Grapefruit seed extract	Good protection from stomach problems including parasites
Calendula cream	Aids rapid skin repair for cuts and sores
Tea tree oil	**Effective if dabbed regularly on athlete's foot. Also 2/3 drops in a glass of water can be gargled to help a sore throat (don't swallow)**
Lavender oil	Excellent for burns and two drops on a pillow aids sleep
Clove oil	**Good for toothache**
Pumpkin seeds	Tasty,high in zinc, and good for fighting stomach parasites
Fennel seeds	**Chewed raw are a good stomach tonic and make a nice tea**
Raw Liquorice sticks	Taste nice, are good for digestion and keeping teeth clean. They are excellent placebo for giving up smoking
Raw garlic	**Excellent for the immune system and general health, a little lime juice in drinking water helps to neutralise the smell**
Herbal teas	Pericon, mint(menta) and spearmint(Hierba buena) teas have a beneficial effect on the digestion.

Nutritional supplements
With the wonderful local fruit and vegetables on offer, it may seem strange to consider taking supplements. However, with unfamiliar food, at first it can be difficult to ensure that the body is getting a good balance of essential nutrients, vitamins and minerals.

10

Clothes and accessories
This is a list of the essential things which should cover most eventualities.

A sun hat	Baseball caps are the hat of choice locally, if wanting to fit in.
A sweater or fleece	**It can get quite cool at night in the highlands.**
Lightweight water proof	Rarely needed for rain but good insulation against the occasional wind and mist in the mountains.
Lightweight trousers	**Preferably a quick drying fabric, as in some places shorts would be considered unsuitable, having Zip pockets make sense.**

NB Whilst cycling, shorts are quite acceptable, its only on arrival at say, a traditional village or church that putting on some trousers at the first oppotunity would be a good idea.

Cotton bandana or Buff	Protection from dust that also keeps necks warm at high altitudes.

In Guatemala and Honduras there are many good quality second hand clothes shops and market stalls, generally called "ropa Americana" if needing cheap extra T-shirts for cycling etc.

Head torches can be useful for cycling, pitching tents and cave exploration.
2 season sleeping bag, cotton or silk liner, and travel mat
Pocket-sized Spanish dictionary
Pocket-knife (cheap Chinese ones of varying quality can be bought locally)
Ear plugs (Tapones) aka sanity savers (can be bought locally from hardware shops)
Waterproof money belt for important documents, mean that swimming alone is safer.
Compass, useful versions clip onto handle bars.
Travel mug is a good way to save plastic waste, when buying drinks from street vendors.
Light weight tent, although in lowland areas a hammock (bought locally) and mosquito net are often more comfortable options.
Strong cotton and a selection of needles
Some "Magic" tape, great for repairing maps, bank notes etc.

Interesting extras
- A football valve to add to your bike pump is excellent way of making friends, football/soccer and basketball are played throughout the region, often with half-flat balls.
- Music breaks down barriers and is great gift to offer if your instrument is small enough
- Things to entertain people, from juggling balls to luminous paints, will help get over gaps in conversation if lacking in Spanish.
- Stickers from home or something similarly cheap and unique as small presents.
- Family photos and home info, very useful in a culture rooted in family life, travelling is often misunderstood, and this link to where you come from is one that all will understand
- A small short wave radio is nice way to keep in touch with home or for learning Spanish.

Bikes
Mountain bikes are the best bet, especially if wanting to get off the beaten track and explore. It's possible to find cheap spare parts everywhere, although the quality is not brilliant.
Bikes with other wheels sizes are harder to find spares for outside the larger towns and cities.

Aluminium frames are strong but don't flex well, so if stored poorly in transport or in a bad accident, they can crack and are very difficult to repair. Steel frames can be welded safely with very basic equipment.

Front suspension is nice for off-roading, although good racks are harder to find to fit them for touring. See panniers section on pg 13

NB Mountain bikes are also easy to sell in an emergency. Most bike shops in larger towns will be interested in a brand name bike.

There are sufficient numbers of quality paved roads serving all the main routes for a touring bike, and road surfaces are being improved every year.

11

Bringing a bike from home
Pick a bike with quality components, but if possible disguise the brand name with tape or paint, as it can attract the wrong sort of attention, and looking after it can become a headache.

Bike check list
- Check wheel rims for flaying, this means they're getting thin, and a potential hazard.
- Replace the chain and brake blocks
- Check the bottom bracket for wear, these days most are sealed units, and if going away for any length of time it's worth replacing. If confident with the maintenance, getting an old style axle and bearings can save lots of hassle, as they are repairable anywhere.
- Check brake and gear cables for fraying.
- Check the headset for play.
Or, if in doubt, get your bike serviced professionally.

Extras
- If possible get wheels with double rims, this will give good protection against buckling, especially with the extra weight of panniers.
- A back block with a 'Granny gear' will mean much less walking in the mountains.
- Get all terrain tyres suitable for paved roads and dirt tracks. There are several varieties of puncture proof tyres worth considering. Giving the locals a laugh whilst repairing a puncture is excellent if the sun is shining, but not so much fun on a cold, mist covered mountain.
NB A budget option is splitting old inner tubes along the seam and using them to line tyres, this gives free increased puncture protection.

Airport procedures for flying with a bike
NB Loosen the pedals a little before reaching the airport.
The standard procedure is to take the pedals off, deflate the tyres and undo the headset, twisting the handle bars through 90 degrees, so the bike can be packed flat. Some airlines may insist on a bag or box as well, these can normally be bought in the airport, but check first.

There is sometimes an extra fee for bike carriage and occasionally the check-in staff may insist on an insurance waiver. This absolves the airline of responsibility in event of damage etc. It's always worth checking these details with the airlines when you buy your ticket.

Buying a bike in Central America
NB Buying a mountain bike suitable for tall people is possible, but isn't easy.
Well-known brands are available in the big cities, although these cater for a small niche market, so the prices are often no cheaper than at home.

There are shops in most towns selling new (heavy)mountain bikes costing about $100. In Mexico cheap and very heavy full-suspension bikes are all the rage, in Belize cool cruiser style bikes are the most popular, and in Guatemala and Honduras standard mountain bikes. Mexican brands such as Benotto are generally reasonable quality, although even this brand has been counterfeited. Vecesa, Vetta, Bacini or Mayatour brands from Guatemala and Honduras are just about passable for most touring, but not for serious off-roading. The advantage is they can be repaired anywhere by local bike mechanics, and don't attract the wrong sort of attention.
NB There is only a limited second hand market, very occasionally shops with uncollected repairs and cycle hire companies sell off bikes.

Tools and bike accessories
There are several different multi-tools on the market, go for quality. One should include:
● A chain link extractor (This will be the first thing to break on a cheap tool)
● Allen (Hex) Key set
● Bike spanners, 8 9, 10, 11, 12mm
● Screwdriver, and a positive (Phillips) head driver
Also...
● Removable lights and/or a head torch.
● A helmets is very sensible for the off-roading sections.
● A basic lock.
● Strong front and back racks with bungee cords
● A 15mm spanner for removing pedals, this is necessary if flying with a bike.
● Pliers, with cutting edge for cables etc
● A couple of old toothbrushes are very useful to clean chains and sprockets
● Pump, Tyre levers and puncture repair kit

Maintenance, spotting potential problems and emergency repairs
● Oil the chain regularly, either carry a small bottle or stop at a garage and ask for a discarded car oil bottle, there is usually just enough left in the bottom for a bike chain. Shortening a broken chain is straightforward with the right tool (although the tools are easy to break if not aligned properly with the chain link)
● If the crank starts to creak, check for sideways play. In normal circumstances it can take a while to disintegrate completely, but with the dust, heat and humidity, it might only last a couple of days. To get a new sealed unit will mean a trip to the nearest city.
● Check the brake alignment regularly, especially if putting your bike on and off buses, if

there are black marks on the walls of your tyres, the brake blocks may have been knocked out of alignment. One of the nastiest and annoying things to happen is to have brake block gradually eat away at the wall of a tyre, leading to a blow out.

If the worst does happens a thick piece of cardboard inserted in the tyre may stop the inner tube from bulging through. With a bit more time, it is possible to sew up split tyres, cross-stitch works best. Use a strong needle and thick thread and don't try to pull the stitches too tightly.

- Check brake blocks regularly for excessive wear, replace well before the metal starts to become exposed! The warning signs are obvious with a metallic sound as the brakes are applied. If left, the brakes will eat into your rims, which will gradually flay, before eventually collapsing.
  If the worst happens! Remove the tyre from the offending wheel, and bind the split area tightly, electrical tape works fine. Replace the tube and tyre, the brake will have to be disabled on that wheel.
- Check cables regularly for flaying. Broken cables can be tied together in an emergency, if the break is in an uncovered section, reef knots work well. This depends on having spare cable at the brake or derraileur end. Once re-attached, try the brakes hard, and re-tension the cable, as the knot will shrink.
- If wheel becomes slightly buckled, a spoke key can bring it true again. This can take a little practice, try not over tighten one spoke, small turns over a longer stretch of spokes will retain the wheels strength. Even a badly buckled wheel can be repaired temporarily to make the bike rideable. Take the wheel off, stand on it or beat the buckled section on the ground until straightish, then use the spoke key. The brake will sometimes have to be disabled.
- Stuffing leaves or grass into tyres works as an emergency puncture repair, although the bike will still be difficult to ride if carrying panniers.

NB There are bike mechanics everywhere, they aren't noted in the text because almost every settlement will have one. Ask for the Taller de bicicletas.

Panniers
NB VERY IMPORTANT. Always bring panniers from home, cheap racks are available locally, but good panniers can't be bought for love or money.

Front or back panniers or both?
This is purely a personal issue, depending on how much you want to carry. If at all possible try to keep your luggage down to two panniers, perhaps with a tent and sleeping bag strapped on the other rack, this inevitably means compromising a little with what you take, but it is worth it. Try to buy panniers that are waterproof, and have minimal zips and extra pockets. Canoe style roll tops work well and are surprisingly secure, as not many people can work out how to open them quickly.

The personal preference of most people who have tried different ways of packing a bike is to have more weight on the front, as it seems more balanced,

Having more weight on the front
Advantages – Front and rear tyre wear is more even. It means you can see your panniers when pushing the bike through streets i.e no nasty surprises of things going missing. and psychologically some find it easier to think of pushing something up a hill, than pulling it.
Disadvantages – The low-rider style racks don't give much ground clearance for rocks, grass tussocks and undergrowth on off-road sections. It also makes the steering heavier, although

this can be an advantage as well, once used to it.

Having more weight on the back
Advantages – there is a much wider range of very strong racks available and more panniers are usually specifically designed for them. It's difficult to go over the handle-bars, if hitting the front brake too hard.
Disadvantages – When stopping for a moment in a crowded place, things very occasionally can go missing, without being noticed. The rear tyre wears relatively quickly.

General cycling tips

Hill and mountain climbing
- Use toe clips or cycling shoes, by using different muscles, they increase climbing power.
- Get a back gear block with a 'granny gear' (32 or 34 teeth).
- Don't try to attack the climb, start slowly and find a steady comfortable rhythm.
- Try to stay in the saddle, standing up will use a lot more energy.
- If it's too much, try for a ride in a pick-up or bus!
- Don't try to climb hills for about an hour after eating.

Dealing with dogs
This is an occasional problem, mainly close to small villages where local dogs can form small packs. Single dogs are unlikely to attack viciously, unless you accidently wander onto property they're guarding.

The first advice is not to panic, stop and put your bike between you and the dog(s). They are very unlikely to do more than bark, they've been kicked too many times!! Normally someone within earshot will come to help, if not:

Bending down (as) to pick up stones will normally send them running. Actually throwing them works very quickly. Or developing a very loud confident shout, Oiiiii !!!!! or similar, will usually stop a dog in it's tracks.

If the worst happens and you are bitten, seek medical attention as quickly as possible.

High altitude cycling
- The weather is critical at high altitudes as the wind is stronger, rain and mist can be prolonged, and surprisingly in this region, it can get cold.
- The human body is less efficient at high altitudes, so until used to the terrain, plan shorter journeys.
- Always have a contingency plan for weather changes, carrying waterproofs and food, finding shelter (may need some Spanish) or making camp.
- Always carry enough water and some supplies of high energy food, Granola (muesli) is a good example and can be bought locally from most supermarkets.

Cycling at night is quite a buzz, there are areas in the lowland jungle where the fireflies are so thick that lights are almost not needed. Ask locally for advice on safety, as areas safe by day are sometimes off-limits at night.

Alternative transport
Time can be very much of the essence, so taking buses or pick-ups through less interesting areas can give time to enjoy the more beautiful journeys at greater leisure.
Pick-ups are often used in rural areas as taxis and communal goods transport. If labouring up a mountain road, exhausted, hurt, or with bike damage, the possibility of flagging one down is

a useful back-up. The amount to be paid is normally similar to the bus, and depending on how full the pick-up is, a little extra for the bike.

Buses are generally good about taking bicycles, normally there is a baggage allowance per passenger of 25kg (50lb), whether this includes a bike can be the subject of lengthy arguments, but usually it doesn't. Paying 50% extra is reasonable, especially if the conductor has put your bike on top of a bus, but it's worth some good natured haggling if double the standard fare is asked for.

There are a few buses where carrying bikes is awkward, due to the llack of roofracks and the luggage compartment being too small. An effort is usually made to fit the bike in somewhere, even over the back row of seats (though this will carry an extra charge). In some rural areas, there are only one or two buses a day and they usually leave very early. Almost all transport links wind down at dusk.

Up to date information sources
- The news network passed on by fellow travellers' is usually pretty reliable, although check stories a couple of times before rushing off.
- The Peace Corps, missionaries and other volunteers are a very useful source of information especially in the remoter areas. They rarely have much money so some form of barter is usually gratefully received. Remember that they are working, and may not have much time to spare.
- The Internet is accessible from every medium sized town and getting increasingly cheaper per hour. Official government travel advice websites provide very useful health and safety information
- Local government offices can be very helpful, however some spanish will normally be required.
- Local tourist magazines like Honduras Tips, Yucatan today etc, occasionally have articles on interesting new destinations, or attractions. They also have many very useful maps.
- Asking locals is often the best way to find out useful information, but be aware that town/city folk often have exaggerated views of potential threats in the countryside, mainly through ignorance. The latin mentality is often to give any answer, usually over cautious, rather than say they don't know. In some circumstances a hand drawn map can be very useful, asking someone to do this for you isn't difficult. Some of the maps make good souvenirs. The best people to ask for route info are pick-up and bus drivers.
- Police stations will usually have good quality large scale maps within their offices. They may be suspicious of your motives so it's important to be able to explain why you want to look at them.
- Tourist offices offer poor quality maps, but they are better than nothing.

Accommodation
Specific accommodations are not listed, this is partly due to the research time, partly space. It's been assumed that cyclists will have the confidence to ask basic questions and directions (see the Spanish phrase section at the back of the book). Checking out the options on a bike is usually quick and painless. Gentle bargaining is not unreasonable, especially if there is a good choice. In smaller towns and villages it has been noted in the text whether or not there is any official accommodation on offer.

Hospedajes, pensions, posadas and hotels
NB Always ask to see your room first before agreeing to take it
In towns, more comfortable hotels are usually dotted around the main plaza, the cheapest accommodation is usually around or near the market or bus station, however these can be

noisy, dirty and not very secure. However, most are well looked after, but basic. The door lock is often only a cheap padlock, so if on a tight budget it's worth bringing a quality spare padlock with you. The smaller towns or villages may only have one cheap hotel(hospedaje) and the bathrooms are usually communal.

In hot low lying areas a fan or air conditioning (check how noisy it is) will be worth the extra for a good nights sleep. A hammock outside can be more pleasant than a room without either.

In some areas, water is rationed, only being usable for a few hours a day. Try not to be wasteful, particularly near the end of the dry season. Taps are often left on to fill giant basins, called pilas, which act as a water source for rest of the day. There is an etiquette to using these as having clean water is important. There are often different containers for getting water out of the pila depending on whether you're washing dirty hands or dishes and clothes.

Hot (warmish) showers, throughout the region are mostly with an electrified shower head, these can vary in quality, but they all operate best with a low water pressure, be careful of bare wires!

Nearly all establishments will let you have the bike in your room.

There's rarely a need to book in advance and often it's not possible to. The only times when its likely to be an issue are Semana Santa (easter) and over Christmas. Although, if wanting to stay at one of the Mexican hostels in Isla Mujeres, Cancun or Playa Carmen, then booking is advisable especially if wanting a base having just flown in. It's easiest on the Net at **www.homecasa.net**

Camping and sleeping out
There are very few private camp sites, although some hotels and hostals allow camping or hammock slinging in their grounds. National parks have some dedicated camping areas, although very often they have been neglected.

In remote areas, camping out or slinging a hammock, is best done discreetly, this means out of view, not pitching up until dusk, and rising early. Ask permission of the landowner if possible, or if near a small village, go to the largest house and ask the headman. There are football pitches everywhere, perfect for camping, although there may well be games quite early on Sunday.

Another option in bad weather is to ask for shelter, go to the largest house in the nearest village, and try to explain your situation. Offer to pay as much as a hospedaje would be, for the bed or hammock space and any food.

Food and drink
The normal range of north American food is available in most towns, however the local Mayan cuisine based around maize, whilst not exactly adventurous, is nourishing and cheap. Wheat based foods are also widely available. Bread, called pan francis if unsweetened, pan dulce if with sugar, and biscuits are usually sold from bakers by the unit currency i.e 6 for a Quetzal.

Tortillas
One of the most endearing sounds of this region is of tortillas being made by hand. It's rare in Mexico as mechanised tortillerias, using subsidised maize flour, produce vast numbers of incredibly cheap and bland tortillas. In countries further south, maize production is still predominately a local thing, and tortillas bought in markets have a much greater variety of textures, tastes and colours. Tortillas are usually sold by the unit currency i.e 5 for a Peso.

Beans, (and sometimes eggs), rice, and chilli (frijoles, heuvos, arroz and chili)
This is the food of the masses for the entire region, and can bought anywhere from the tiniest village to the capital cities. In emergencies, a few tortillas and some beans can be bought

from almost any house on asking. Although it would be wise to ensure the family have enough for themselves.

There are several different types of maize and beans used for this meal, and the taste, quality and price will vary from place to place. Meat or just the stock is sometimes added as well. Asking for some raw onion (Cebollo crudo) to be mixed with the beans, not only varies the taste, it's also excellent for maintaining good health. Salad is often based around grated cabbage with avocado, onion and tomato.

NB Vegetarians, manteca is animal fat and often used in the refrying of beans and other food. Meat (carne) means red meat, Chicken (pollo) and fish (pescaro) are thought of differently.

Roadside food possibilities
These small shops, often no more than huts, usually only sell canned drinks, sweets, cigarettes, and assorted snacks. In agricultural areas there are occasional fruit and vegetable stalls, selling the seasons harvest.

Street vended hot drinks
A nice way to start or finish the day is with arroz con leche or mosh (!) These thick hot drinks are made with rice or oats with milk, sugar or honey and loads of cinamom. Atole blanca, is liquified maize meal, usually served in a bowl with chilli, a few beans and some seasoning, not everyone's idea of food, but very cheap. Sometimes there are sweeter chocolate or banana flavoured versions of the above. Using your own travel mug saves hygiene worries where mugs are only rinsed between use.

Street vended cold drinks
Natural water based drinks (refrescos), fruit juice (jugos) and smoothies with or without milk (liquardos) are delicious. It's normal to add sugar, if not having quite such a sweet tooth ask for your drink "sin azucar". They are normally made with pure water (agua pura), but it may be worth checking. The usual mix of canned or bottled soft drinks are available everywhere.

Examples of street vended and market snacks
Tamales – These are cooked maize surrounding meat, beans, greens or sugar, wrapped in a banana leaf. Sometimes they're toasted, sometimes steamed.
Tostadas – Toasted tortillas topped with beans, avocado, salad, meat or cheese
Plantains, fried or grilled with cream
Sopa – Soup usually mixed vegetable, with some lumps of meat floating in it.

Local fruit and vegetables
There are several varieties of well known fruit, like bananas, mangos and avocados that are quite different in terms of size, shape and taste to those bought in supermarkets at home. It's also worth experimenting with some of the unknown fruits on offer, although seasonal favourites like green (unripe) mangos, usually sold sliced in a bag with salt, can be hard on delicate stomachs.

Peeling fruit is the safest way to eat it, although washing things like berries in water with a few drops of iodine (left for twenty minutes) should kill most nasties.

Buying things from the markets is done in pounds (libros). 1kg = 2.2Libros, or more often for small amounts by the unit currency, e.g 2 Mangos for a Peso.

Alcohol
Every country takes great pride in producing it's own beverages, they are usually weak lager like beers, thirst quenching, but not very exciting. Occasionally darker beers are available that

have a little more taste, like Gallo Moza in Guatemala.

Wines, unless imported (and expensive) are not worth bothering with, being very poor quality and sugary.

Spirits are mainly sugar cane based, like aguadiente (popular in Mayan ceremonies), Ron (rum) and illicit alcohol called cusha.

Coffee

Some of the worlds finest coffee is produced in this region, although nearly all is exported, so it's only possible to get a taste of the real thing in the cafes of San Cristobal, Antigua and other wealthier towns. Elsewhere many people use cheap instant granules.

Honduras is the exception as it doesn't have world recognition for being a producer of quality coffee, so the excellent local beans are used everywhere.

Home made ices

These tasty home-made cheap treats are a great way to cool off. They're normally advertised on the side of houses or shops and nearly every settlement will have someone who makes them for a bit of extra cash, though sometimes you have to ask for them. Flavours include artificial possibilities, like Kool aid. Natural flavours include coconut, pineapple, mango, berry, banana and other fruits, sometimes mixed with with milk, chocolate or nuts. Unusual combinations like milk, cornflakes and nuts are common.

They are called different things in different places, Topogios, Helados, Palletas, Vasitos etc. Sometimes they are sold on sticks, sometimes in a small plastic bag. *Are they safe?* Well they are generally made by mothers for children, so they will have safety in mind, but it may be worth asking if they are made with purified water (agua pura).

Chocobananos are what they say they are, frozen bananas on a stick drenched in chocolate, absolutely gorgeous!

Water

There are many different ways of making water safe to drink, and what is for sure is that no-one wants to get ill.

The standard advice is to only drink purified bottled water, although this does mean throwing away a lot of plastic. Bags of pure water, (bolsas de agua pura) can be bought in almost every village (although harder to come by in Mexico). They come in half litre size are very cheap and usually chilled, bite or cut the corner off and empty into your old water bottle.

However, cycling can be sweaty thing, and in rural areas it's often easier to buy Coke than purified water, so a compromise has to be reached:

- One of the easiest options is a personal water filter, these are relatively cheap, but the filter cartridges do need replacing regularly.
- Boiling water is an effective method of sterilisation, although for the quantities needed over a day, is very time consuming.
- Iodine can be used to purify water, although the taste is not good. It's important to wait twenty minutes before drinking and it shouldn't be used as a long term solution.
- Slightly more risky is to use some common sense. Taking water from mountain streams and springs is often the only option in remote areas. Although never drink unpurified water from an open source if it's likely there are animals or humans using the water higher up, even then take from running water rather than still.

Rural development schemes to provide piped spring water to communities are being started up all the time, often funded by foreign agencies. The water is often better than bottled water, so asking a household with a private tap to is ok, public taps always carry a small risk.

Water in many places is only available through a tap for a few hours a day. This gets more common towards the end of the dry season. People have large basins called pilas to collect as much as possible when it's running. It's important to respect local etiquette when taking water from them, in order to keep the rest as clean as possible.

Travelling alone

Meeting fellow travellers can be a bit harder when cycling, which for some is a bonus!! But if wanting some company, there are several places where travellers naturally seem to gather to relax, mentioned in the text.

Travelling alone is sometimes considered strange by rural people who only know a family orientated lifestyle. Taking pictures of home, friends and family helps to create understanding. Having a reason for travelling can also make the idea seem less strange to some locals. It could be fictitious, but voluntary work or learning Spanish would make some sense.

For single women these attitudes are amplified, and for an easy life, having a fictitious partner can be a good idea, along with a bit of evidence like a ring and/or a photo.

In many parts of all Central America it's quite normal for cyclists to whistle at each other when passing! (this might be differently interpreted for women!) Every area seems to have a different style, it's nice to respond with your own whistle and a comforting form of communication especially if lacking Spanish skills.

Common issues and avoiding problems

19

General precautions

- When ordering food, or buying anything, always agree the price first. In some situations it can seem awkward. However it does save the occasional embarrassing experiences of someone coming up with a ridiculous price later on. Having eaten the food or enjoyed an excursion, it's not a strong bargaining position.
- On narrow roads in the countryside, the vehicle ascending a hill has the right of way, this is worth bearing in mind if wanting to downhill at speed.
- In rural areas, transport and shops usually start shutting down when the sun sets, even in small towns this is often the case unless there's a market the following day
- Taking photos is for most people, an essential part of travelling, however, in some places buying postcards is a more sensitive option. If in doubt ask permission of the people concerned.
- Avoid voicing strong political or religious opinions, unless sure of your company. Declaring yourself an atheist for example might lead to confusion and misunderstandings in some circumstances.

Annoyances

Old diesel vehicles – Can have you gasping with clouds of black exhaust, especially on an uphill, and is part of the reason for this guide encouraging avoidance of main roads.
Dusty roads – Are generally fine until a vehicle passes at speed, with plumes of dust spiralling behind. A bandana and sunglasses can make it bearable, the worst roads are noted within the text.
Litter – This is perhaps the most unpleasant annoyance, cyclists get the pleasure of seeing what local residents do with their litter, notedly roadside dumps a km or so outside settlements . The philosophy is out of sight, out of mind, and where the stuff ends up seems irrelevant. The dumps are sometimes set on fire, to reduce the volume.

Common fears

Snakes – Love them or hate them, the nearest most will get to see them is squashed on the road, or in pieces on a path, having been macheted to death.

Machetes – These big knives are carried and used everywhere, for everything from agriculture to building and can be a cause for alarm at first. Many men use a sheaf, and on some buses they have to be handed to the driver when boarding.

Gangs – There have been many highly publicised problems over the last few years, throughout the whole region. The culture is one of the less desirable US imports. Crack downs do seem to be having some effect, but at a violent cost. Re-integrating gang members into the wider community will be a real challenge for the politicians in the future. The grafitti for different gangs is everywhere, but in reality it's as much as most travellers will see of them.

Theft and robbery – Common issues, but it is possible to minimise the risks. This region has been well travelled, and the main problem areas are known and have been covered in the text. Asking locals regularly for advice, will give confidence, and is the best way to find out if any area is potentially dangerous.

Earthquakes – Can be very unnerving if never experienced before. They do occur regularly, often without being noticed. The motion is usually from side to side, if inside head quickly for a door way or outside. If the big one happens, be aware that law and order may temporarily be a serious issue.

Roaming farm animals – In rural areas can be an occassional surprise, however the large horned cattle are peaceful, and will lumber slowly out of the way. Donkeys, mules and horses need a little more care, stay clear of potential kicks from back legs.

Bad drivers – Generally, most drivers are quite respectful of cyclists, however, they do sometimes pass other cars more with trust in God, than good driver judgement! This can be particularly unnerving if both cars are coming toward you, The only sensible advice is to be aware and avoid the busier roads where this is more common.

Bus drivers, particularly in Guatemala have a reputation, and unfortunately some do expect cyclists to pull over when they sound their horns, however they are mostly good drivers, and will wait to pass.

General hostility – The people of this region are on the whole friendly to tourists. However, occasionally there can appear to be mild hostility, this is sometimes vocalised by the local kids, Although is often done in fun as well, shouts of "gringo" are common!

Some are aggrieved by bad treatment they have had working in north America, some might be jealous of an expensive bike etc. Any aggression should be taken seriously, but use common sense, don't over react, they may have had a hard day at work. If a friendly smile is ignored, then it is better to move on.

Travel ethics

This isn't a sermon! but it does make sense to support the poorest, by buying local products and food. The markets are the easiest places to do this. Haggling is fun, but pushing it too hard can really upset people who are well aware of the wealth differences. The comparison of the equivalent price in US Dollars is sometimes given as a sarcastic response.

Culture

History

A little outside the remit of this book, but it can be interesting, there are many books available in English and Spanish, as well as a wealth of information on the Net.

The Mayan peoples of this region had warriors, as well as highly developed sciences and

arts. It really is quite incredible to think how a few hundred Spaniards on horseback could have eventually come to conquer this region.

More recent history has some seen civil wars, many caused by cold war tensions, others due to indigenous repression going back centuries.

31st December 2012 is being mooted, much as 2000 was, as a time of great spiritual significance. In the ancient Mayan way of understanding time, the 31st December 2012 will be the ending of one giant cycle and the beginning of another. Some see this as a potential disaster (the end of the world etc), others great change, what is for sure, is that there will be increasing numbers of people trying to make some money out of it, along with the gurus etc.

Sport

There are soccer pitches and basketball courts everywhere, sometimes perched in the most amazing places, and impromtu games are not unusual. Asking to take part in a game is a great way of getting to know people, without needing language skills.

Architecture and building

Colonial – Town and city cobbled streets were normally laid out in a uniform grid pattern, and usually along the lines of the main compass points. The stone built cathedrals and churches reflected the wealth of a particular area, quite large churches can be found in tiny villages, that had wealthy agricultural production. They were often built using the stone from destroyed Mayan buildings

Traditional rural – Adobe buildings made of clay and straw wedged into blocks are everywhere, although post-earthquake re-inforced concrete is becoming more prevalent particularly in Guatemala. Pan tiles have likewise been replaced by corrugated iron, due to cost and the weight which can be dangerous in tremors. The rural buildings in Honduras are the exception with many roofed with in traditional pan tiles, the cost is small treeless areas centred around the large kilns used in their making.

The Yucatan Maya have beautiful pole and thatch huts, often surrounded by rough stone walls. These are everywhere, and the result of centuries of stone-picking from nearby fields.

Palapas are open palm covered shelters suitable for hammocks. **Cabanas,** literally cabins, are often made of bamboo and usually palm covered although the word is often used for any one room structure. They're both found only on the coasts and lowlands, where the temperatures are higher.

Mayan ancient buildings – The impressive stone pyramids and palaces of this culture were normally made from limestone. They don't have quite same degree of masonic precision found in Egypt or Peru, however they were well built, and their construction would have employed a whole class of workers and artisans, whose skills now seem to be lost.

There are ruins constantly being uncovered, and conservation efforts to maintain and improve the appearance of existing ruins are an ongoing concern.

National parks and ruin sites

Nearly all have an entrance fee of some kind, specific prices have not been given, as they are subject to inflation. However, entrance fees are rarely more than US$5 or $6, they have risen gradually over the last 5 years, but have not been so prone to the price hikes of other private trips and excursions. There are often discounts, so taking an international student card is worthwhile.

Gentle haggling at less visited ruins and attractions, can work sometimes.

Wildlife
The famous jaguars, quetzals and manatees of this region are good at hiding, and it will be a very special day if one of these rare creatures is actually seen. But on the whole, cycling is an excellent way of seeing wildlife, because it's quiet and relatively quick animals and birds often don't have time to hide, the most usual birdlife seen is:

● The vultures and occasionally eagles soaring on the midday thermals.
● The tuneful long-tailed blackbirds (AKA Great tailed Grackles) are full of character.
● White egrets picking through the grassland next to grazing cattle
Bursts of colour, yellow, green or red as a surprised bird flies out of the undergrowth are common. Butterflies of all sizes and colours drift across the road. The massive blue moon butterfly is one difficult to miss. The beautiful tree blossoms of orange, purple, red and other colours, brightens a journey. White Monja blanca flowers are grown in the mountains, they are a national symbol in Guatemala.

Toucans and spider monkeys can be seen in numbers at the Tikal ruins. Howler monkeys are often heard but not seen, the easiest places to catch a glimpse is at the Palenque ruins. Turtles and Caymens can be seen at places like Monterico in Guatemala. Quetzals can be seen in the forests around Fuentes Georgina (nr Xela), Senahu, or at the Mary Davy Quetzal reserve. The best times to see wildlife are the early mornings, at other times some forest areas can seem eerily quiet.

MEXICO

Immigration – These are a formality for North Americans, Australasians and members of the European Union involving filling out a simple tourist card. Hang onto this whilst in Mexico, and hand it in when leaving the country.

If flying into Cancun, it's generally better not to put Chiapas as your official destination on your tourist card, as the airport officials can't understand why anyone would want to go there.

A new tourist tax of $20 (liable to increase with time) is payable to a local bank before leaving the county.

People – The majority are Mestizos (of latin and indigenous blood), a derivation of which gave this country it's name. There are also several different groups of Mayan peoples, as well as a small number of Lacandon.

Language – Spanish is spoken (almost) universally, although in many areas Mayans still use their languages for every day communication.

Money and costs – Mexican Pesos are more stable these days, although like every other Central American economy the exchange rate fluctuates with the US dollar.

Mexico is growing quickly economically, so prices will inevitably rise as well. It's certainly no longer a shoestring destination, although away from the tourist centres it's still possible to travel very cheaply.

Roads – Main highways are in good condition, and well maintained. New intercity roads are being made, notedly from Merida toward Felipe Carillo Puerto. Minor roads are less predictable and can have occasional deep pot holes. Dirt tracks are rapidly being paved, although there are good trails around San Cristobal in Chiapas.

Alternative transport – There are different classes of buses between all towns, at reasonable prices. Officially there's a charge for bicycles, normally half fare, although this seems to be rarely applied, usually only when the buses are full at holiday times. The buses have a speed cap of 95km/h, which will explain the occasional buzzer going off from the driver's cab.

General tips and observations

- There are military check points at all the state boundaries, and on roads leading to the Guatemalan and Belizean borders, this is to try and halt the tide of economic migrants and drug trafficking.
- An up-to-date map of the Yucatan can be found on walls of Pemex gas stations, It has all the new roads marked, unfortunately there aren't versions for sale.
- The Mexican hostel network now provides cheap pleasant accommodation in nearly all the main tourist centres. Booking is straight forward through the website at **www.homecasa.net**
- Rough camping is generally acceptable, but if near a settlement, make an effort to ask at the local palacio municipal. Nearly all enquiries will be referred there, as they like to know what's going on.
- Visiting ruins and museums on Sundays is no longer free for tourists.

The Yucatan Peninsular

Being predominately flat, cycling is easy, although the distances and intense midday heat are important factors to take into account. It's a great area to get fit, either prior to more strenuous cycling in the mountains or as a one or two week holiday.

The countryside is predominately covered with a low canopy of trees, ranches and mixed agriculture. This means that birds and other treetop creatures are more easily visible and at some times of year there are large numbers of butterflies. The colonial splendour of the old towns, and impressive Mayan ruins mean there are plenty of opportunities to stop and enjoy the local culture.

The scenery on some of the main highways can become monotonous, making bus trips a sensible option. On the less travelled rural routes there are many idyllic traditional Mayan settlements with pole and thatch buildings, surrounded by dry stone walls.

NB The wind predominates from the southeast, and with the relative lack of shelter from the low lying vegetation, cycling eastwards can be hard work.

The cycling highlights include:
- Tulum to Punta Allen and through the Sian Kaan NP to Sta Philippe Carillo.
- The Puuc hills, including Uxmal, the Puuc ruin sites and the Loltun caves.
- Peto to Valladolid or vice versa.

An example of a 2 week touring route around Cancun:
Cancun-Tulum (Beaches coba and Tulum ruins)-Felipe Carillo Puerto (Sian Kaan Reserve)-Puuc region (Uxmal and other ruins)-Merida (ruins, hammocks and colonial splendour)-Izamal (Pristine colonial town)-Valladolid (Chichen Itza and Ek Balam ruins)-Cancun (Isla Mujeres)

An example of a 1 week touring route around Merida:
Merida-Convent route-Puuc hills (Uxmal ruins etc)-Peto-Valladolid-Izamal-Tixkokob-Merida

Cancun airport to Cancun, 18km – The road out of the airport joins the main north-south highway after a 3km. Turn left to head north toward Cancun, the road is uninteresting and can be busy, but has plenty of space for cycling. It leads straight into downtown, passing the bus station. With time it's much nicer to explore the hotel zone loop (30km), continue straight over the highway, it is well signed. This road has good coastal views and access to local beaches.

There are buses to Cancun from close to the front of the main terminal, although there isn't much space for bikes, and there would be a big surcharge for carrying them.

The ITMB map shows a dubious road from the airport to the East-West Highway

Cancun airport toward Playa Carmen/Tulum – If wanting to head south straight away, follow the road out of the airport and right turn onto the 4-lane highway. It's not the nicest introduction to cycling in the area, although there is plenty of space at the side of the road. Buses south can be hailed from the side of this highway, although with a bike it's not easy to persuade drivers to stop. So, either cycle to Cancun or Puerto Morale and take a bus from the terminal there.

☞ see p.33 or routes south along the **Caribbean coast** to **Chetumal**.

Cancun

This city is the main package tourist centre of the area, catering for the one and two week holiday crowds. There are dozens of hotels on a 30km loop that stretches from the city centre around a lagoon on the coast. The resort has many clubs and is starting to attract younger generations.

24

In the city the fruit and vegetable market, along with several cheap comedors, is 2 blocks west of Ave Tulum a few blocks north of the bus terminal. The market for leather goods, clothes and cheap bits and pieces is along Ave Chichen Itza, starting at the junction with Ave Tulum. The tourist information office is again on Ave Tulum at the junction with Ave Coba. It isn't much help at present, and seems to be closed sporadically.

There are buses to almost every destination on the Yucatan, Chiapas and up to Mexico City. The large terminal is easily found on Ave Tulum (at the junction where Ave Uxmal branches off). There are a couple of hostels 2 blocks north, and many hotels in the vicinity.

Cancun to Isla Mujeres – Passenger ferries go from Puerto Juarez, 3km north east of the town centre. Follow Ave Tulum north, until it meets with Ave Lopez Portillo, turn right, this road leads down to the port. There are fast and slow boats, bikes can be transported on both, however the slow boat is predictably a lot cheaper and a relaxing journey on a calm day (it doesn't run during high winds). A more expensive car and truck ferry goes from Punta Sam 4km further north of Puerto Juarez.

Isla Mujeres
This touristy, but laid-back island, is only a short boat ride away from Cancun, and a nice place to relax away from the bustle of the city, especially whilst acclimatising.

Accommodations from hostel dormitories and camping to hotels are available in the small town by the port. There are many restaurants, a small market, a bank and some excellent beaches within walking distance. It's a nice ride down to the southern tip of the island (along the eastern coast) with good views.

NB Camping out on the beach is not a good idea, the local tourist police run regular patrols.

25

Cancun–Merida
Cancun to Valladolid, 180km – From the town centre follow signs to Merida, the road out of Cancun is busy and it takes 20km to leave all the town behind, some traffic is then lost onto the toll highway.

The road is in reasonable condition, but isn't very wide. for the volume of traffic. There are a couple of sections of mild undulation, and only occasional shade from road side trees. There are many speed bumps (Topes) around the many small villages on this road and they work well in slowing the traffic down. Upgraded sections go around some of the older settlements like X-Can which have large limewashed churches, but are only worth exploring for food/rest breaks away from the road. Chemax nearer Valladolid has a little more to offer.

The countryside in between has widespread agriculture, scrub vegetation, with occasional low canopy forest. Regular roadside shops are good for supplies although the selection of accommodation is poor, so camping discretely is good option.

Taking a bus out of Cancun is recommended for those with limited time.

Valladolid
This colonial town can be a very pleasant place to acclimatise being relaxed and tourist friendly. Accommodations are mostly within 2 blocks of the square, and there are many comedors and restaurants in the same area. The bus station is a couple of blocks west.

Tourist information is next to the impressive cathedral, try to pick up a copy of the free tourist magazine 'Yucatan Today', for useful maps and up-to-date information.

The Cenote Zaci, is a couple of blocks East and North of the main square, and worth a visit. The covered market is a bit further in the same direction.

NB There is a new highway around the northern side of Valladolid

SIDE TRIPS

The cenote Dzitnup, 5km – There is now a 3km cycle path, from the western edge of town alongside the road to Merida. At the signed junction for Dzitnup, turn left and continue along the twisting road for 2km, coming to a parking area surrounded by trinket stalls. The entrance fee is cheap and the lights do make it particularly impressive. Swimming in the cavern, is a treat in the heat of the day. Camping is possible on the football pitch on the other side of the road. A new cenote has been opened up on the same road, and is now open for visitors.

NB There are plans in the pipeline for a major tourist development at the cenote Dzitnup

The Ek Balam ruins, 25km – These ruins north of town are worth the trip, they have a small amount of surrounding forest, are quiet and climbing some of the buildings gives some excellent views.

The road goes north from the centre of town, if in doubt ask for the way to Temazon. After crossing the highway the route is very quiet, unfortunately the scrub vegetation gives little shade. The village of Temazon, just over half way, has a few shops and a couple of comedors in the market, take some supplies and water as there is only a very basic snack selection at the ruins.

Alternatively put your bike on the bus to Tizimin, and ask to be dropped at the junction to the ruins, it's another 6km. Cycling back to Valladolid in the early evening is very pleasant.

If heading west from Valladolid – The route to the Coba ruins goes from close to the Quintana Roo/ Yucatan boundary at Neuvo X-can. This is a quiet road passing a few small villages, it's a good cut through to Tulum which cuts out Cancun.

Valladolid to Rio Lagartos, 200km round trip – The main reason to go is for the flamingos and other birds. Tours can be organised at the waterfront of this sleepy fishing village, try to meet up with fellow travellers' to keep the costs of the launch ride down. As a side trip, taking a bus (with or without bike) is a reasonable option, it requires a change halfway in the small town of Tizimin.

Heading due north from Valladolid as for the Ek Balam ruins, there are a few gentle climbs. Onwards the route hasn't been cycled, although the scenery is similar to the rest of the Yucatan, being mainly low forest and scrubby vegetation. The traffic is quiet and the longer gaps between settlements, mean it's important to take some supplies.

In Rio Lagartos there are a few rooms to rent and a hotel, unexplored sandy tracks into the coastal biosphere reserve could give good cycling.

Valladolid to Izamal (direct), 100km – This old colonial route is quiet and passes through some interesting towns and villages. The road is in reasonable condition, and has been improved to by-pass some villages in places, however there are still a few pot-holes! Whilst mostly flat the road does gently undulate in places, there are very few settlements between the towns marked on the map, so carrying enough water and food is important.

The junction for this shaded road is at the western edge of Valladolid, it crosses the new highway around the town, and then the expressway nearer Uayama. The newer section of road around this traditional village has less tree cover, but there's more shade nearer Tinum(shops) where there are some pretty old buildings. The next section to Dzitas has a few gentle climbs, and this is the only town of any size on the route, and a nice place for a food/meal break. The narrow, partially shaded roads continue to Tunkas(shops), afterwards the countryside gradually opens out and there are more fincas and ranches meaning less shade

There is no official accommodation en-route, although camping discretely with permission is an easy safe option.

☞ Go to p.28 for **Izamal** and onwards

Valladolid to Peto, 110km – If not bothered about visiting the city of Merida then this route is a beautiful alternative to get to the Puuc hills, for Uxmal and other ruins. There is very little traffic, although a daily bus if needing a little help. The paved road undulates through the countryside, and is a pleasure to cycle.

Take the main road west, and turn off after 3km to the cenote Dzitnup. This small road eventually leads to the village of Tekom, where there a few shops and a comedor. Next the route follows the small road to Chibilub (no shops), it may be necessary to ask where this starts from, as a new road has altered traffic priority. There are a few tiny traditional settlements on the way, and some shade from the forest. From there follow the same road to Xuxucab, there's less shade on this section. Turn left, for the next 10km to the larger settlement of Chikindzonot(shops). Then it's another 18km to the unique village of **Ichmul**.

There are two beautiful ruined churches in this tiny village, and another one in use, all massively out of proportion for a village of this size (history must have some stories!). There are a couple of shops, and a large open area surrounded by old buildings in front of the churches.

Onwards to Peto, there are more beautiful traditional Mayan settlements, a mixture of scrubby vegetation and some trees along the road side for partial shade.

There are a couple of basic accommodation options in Peto. Onwards to Oxkutzcab the roads are bigger, there are two options; via Tixmhauc, on the new highway (little shade and no places to stop then a cut through on a narrow country road), or via Tzucacab on the older main road. Both routes meet up in the colonial town of Tekax, before continuing to Oxkutzcab

☞ Go to p.29 for the **Puuc region**

Valladolid to Chichen Itza (Piste), 44km – If wanting to cycle toward Merida, the most pleasant route goes direct to Izamal, by-passing the Chichen Itza ruins, but they are easily visited by a bus from Valladolid. The route is much like that from Cancun, an uninteresting straight road with scrubby vegetation, although there are fewer settlements. The Balankche caves are just off the highway 3km from Piste.

Chichen Itza ruins

The functional town of Piste has services for basic needs, but little of interest. There is a mix of accommodation to suit most budgets, from hotels to hammock slinging.

The Chichen Itza ruins are a short 2km walk or ride to the east of town. They are very impressive and certainly worth a visit, although the sheer number of tourists can take a little away from their magnitude.

Chichen Itza (Piste) to Izamal, 70 km – This route is not the most interesting and there is no shade. There are 50km to do on the main highway, which can be broken halfway at the cenote Xotjil, just off the road and great for cooling off in.

Turn right in Kantunil and once over the expressway, the road is much quieter, dotted with a few small settlements, farmland and scrub.

Izamal

This provincial town is lovely destination, not least because of it's colonial architecture, much of it painted in a warm yellow colour, but also it's natural charm. There are several nice places to stay, although the prices may stretch a tight budget. The market is just off the main square, near the church and other beautiful colonial buildings. Substantial ruins are being restored to the north of the main plazas, climbing them offers good views over the town. There are trains which run periodically to Merida, the station is north of the main square.

Izamal to Merida, about 65km – There are some pretty, quiet roads, unmarked on the ITMB map from Citilcum to Titzkokob. This pleasant town has the attraction of being one of the main hammock-making centres. There are several shops, and some haggling will normally be required. Another option is buying direct from the makers, they can be seen in most villages passed through on this route. Nearer Merida the roads become predictably busier and wider, follow the signs to the Zocalo for the city centre.

Merida

This is very much the cultural capital of the peninsula, the one way streets around the centre are bustling, and the tourist office is on the east side of the main square (Zocalo). Maps in the free tourist magazine Yucatan Today, are very useful for navigation in the city and it occasionally has good articles. Copies can be picked up from any large hotel or the tourist office. Accommodation of the cheaper variety can be found around the train station (a few blocks further east of the main square) and also south on the way to the bus stations. There is a wide choice for differing budgets.

There is no central bus terminal, although all the different bus stations are south of the Zocalo, and within a couple of minutes riding.

The Dzibilchaltun ruins, 12km – are worth a visit especially if wanting a fresh water swim in the cenote Xlaca. There are some pleasant, quiet backroads nearby to explore, although getting out of the city still involves dealing with the heavy traffic. Head north east to the suburb of Cholul, and ask directions to Temazon. From there turn right on an unmarked road to the village of Chablekal (shops and food), then turn left ,and it's another 2km to the ruins.

It's possible to camp in the village of Dzibilchaltun behind the local government office. Coming back; either the same way or along the Progresso highway.

Trips to Progresso on the north coast or Celestun for the flamingos, on the east coast, are probably better done as bus day trips.

If heading east from Merida take Calle 65 to get to Tzikokob and the quieter route to Valladolid.

Merida–Campeche

Merida to Uxmal and the Puuc hills about 85km – The most interesting road south is via Kanasin, Acanceh and the Mayapan ruins to Mama, then on to Ticul or Oxkutzcab.
This is also known as the convent route and is one to start early as there are many interesting places to stop.
NB Taking a bus to Acanceh to avoid the city traffic or if wanting to start later, can be a good idea.
To leave Merida, take the Calle 69 east, and follow signs to Kanasin. The road has recently been upgraded and now has plenty of space for cyclists, although offers little shade.
It now by-passes all the following towns and villages:
Acanceh is an unusual town, having pyramid ruins next to the plaza and church, it has a small busy market and the usual food stalls.
Tekoh the next town has an interesting old church and unusual old market building.
Telchquillo is a quiet village which has a nice old church and pretty cenote.
The **Mayapan** ruins are well worth a visit, being interesting, untouristy and offering good views over the surrounding countryside.

Tekit is a lovely town with bags of character.
The detour to **Mama** is well worth it, for the old church, and for the journey there on the more peaceful old road. Onwards there is apparently a track which connects to Mani. The alternative involves doing two sides of a triangle, via Teabo on the new highway.
Mani is a pretty town, with a large church and one simple accommodation option
Onwards there are roads continuing onto Oxkutzcab or Ticul for cheaper, plentiful accommodation options

The Puuc Hills
The quiet roads through these hillsare excellent for cycling as the distances are small, and the lowland forest canopy gives some shade. There are some climbs and undulation, but nothing too strenuous, they make a pleasant change from the rest of the Yucatan.
Places to stay within the region:

Ticul – is being developed for tourism and has several places to stay. If staying in Ticul, the short ride to Mani would make a nice evening side trip.

Oxkutzcab – is less developed for tourism, but has a few basic options for accommodation.

Mani – has a small pension with a couple of rooms to rent.

Santa Elena – has a beautiful big church and a lot of character, there are a couple of comedors on the main square.

The Sacbe campgrounds – are 2km south west of Sta Elena just off the main road toward Holpelchen. They're an extra 14km on the journey from Merida, with a 100m climb out of Ticul, but rewarded with excellent views over the plains below. The camping ground hosts are good sources of up to date local information.

There is also a hospedaje close to the junction of the main road to Uxmal.

Uxmal – these extensive and impressive ruins are well worth making the effort to visit.

For accommodation there are several hotels near these ruins, although they are all reasonably expensive. The closest budget options are in Sta Elena.

Some things to bear in mind:

The tours of the **Loltun caves** are at set times depending on which language is preferred, so if planning to visit it's worth checking locally or in the latest issue of Yucatan Today.

The **Xlapak ruins** can seem a let down compared to the impressiveness of the others.

The admission costs to all sites can knock a hole in daily budgeting. The **Labna, Sayil and Uxmal** ruins are worth paying for, many of the Kabah ruins can be seen from the road.

30

The Puuc Route
Navigation is straight forward using the ITMB map
The route from Oxkutzcab including the Loltun caves, Puuc ruins and Uxmal to Muna is just over 80km, and could be done in one long day. Taking a bus back from Muna to Ticul or Oxkutzcab takes the strain out of the day. (The route could be done either way round.)

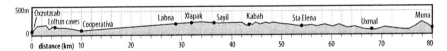

From the back of Oxkutzcab, there is a climb into the hills for a couple of km, the road then undulates passing the Loltun caves, before dropping to the village of Cooperativa (shops). Onwards there's a steady gentle climb for several km through orange orchards and other plantations, until gradually the natural forest takes over. It's about 15km to the Labna ruins, the Xlapak and Sayil ruins are a few km further on in the forested hills.

The junction with the Holpelchen road sometimes has a military checkpoint. Turning right, the

road undulates heavily, passing the Kabah ruins, and the junction for Santa Elena (it's 2km into town for comedors and shops), there's less shade on this road. The undulations continue almost all the way to Uxmal (see below) another 14 Km away.

Onwards to Muna, the road drops and undulates again before climbing over a ridge of the Puuc hills (great for sunsets) and down into the town.

Take plenty of water and supplies, some of the ruin entrance buildings sell refreshments, but there aren't many other shops outside the towns.

Uxmal

These ruins are worth a separate trip if possible, as the site is very impressive and extensive, the number of tourists can't take away from their magnitude and it's easy to spend several hours on the site.

Climbing the Temple of the Magicians is occasionally restricted, although there are several other unrestored pyramids on the site to climb with excellent views over the surrounding countryside and ruins.

There are several hotels near the site, cheaper options are available in Muna and Sta Elena.

The Puuc region–Valladolid

The Puuc region(Oxkutzcab) to Peto, 64km – From Oxkutzcab follow the main road to the town of Tekax, this place is worth a few minutes cycling around, as it has several old colonial buildings in various states of repair. Onwards to Peto are choice of routes. Continue on the same road through Ticum to Tzucacab, then turn left toward Peto.

Alternatively, if wanting to deal with less traffic, there is a very peaceful, partially shaded road to Tixmehuac (ask locally for the right road, it turns off to the left several blocks after the plaza), which then passes through a couple of small villages. From there take the new intercity route which cuts through to the south of Peto (there is no shade on this highway).

Peto – This is a large provincial town, serving a wide area. It has big markets, comedors and church on the edge of a large square.

The onward route toward Felipe Carillo Puerto is unresearched, but appears to have little of interest, there are regular buses if heading in this direction.

Peto to Valladolid, about 110km – from several blocks north of the plaza, take the road toward Ichmul, there are a few interesting traditional Mayan villages en route. The scenery is mainly lowland forest or scrub, with some local agriculture. The road undulates gently in places, and there is partial shade for much of the route.

After about 35km, the first settlement of any size is **Ichmul** (2/3 shops). This village is completely off the tourist trail and stunning in it's decayed grandeur, there are two beautiful ruined churches, and a big open area in front of them surrounded by old colonial buildings. It's worth spending a bit of time wandering around to get a feel for the place.

From Ichmul, follow the road to the larger settlement of Chinkindzonot (shops), keep going and turn right in the next village of Xuxcab. The road then passes through several smaller Mayan settlements, surrounded by thicker forest on the way to the town of Tekom (food and shops). The back roads can then be followed via the cenote Dzitnap to Valladolid.

The Puuc region to Campeche

The Puuc region to Hopelchen, 80km – From Sta Elena, the road undulates past the ruins of Kabah, and through the army checkpoint at the junction of the road toward the other Puuc sites and Oxkutzcab. The road undulates more heavily, through the low canopy forest, and passes under an arch separating the states of Yucatan and Campeche.

The next real sign of civilization is Bolonchen after 40km. The caves to the south of the town are well worth exploring as a break from the sun. Further south there are increasing numbers of clearances for agriculture and more ranches, meaning less shade nearer Holpelchen. *NB Take enough water and food, as opportunities to refill between settlements are limited.*

Hopelchen

This peaceful small town is in the middle of an important agricultural area, members of a nearby community of Mennonite farmers, can often be seen in their blue overalls.
There is one very basic hospedaje if needed and a couple of places to eat.

Hopelchen toward the Calakmul Bioreserve – These unresearched routes could be an interesting diversion, there are some ruin sites for which cycling is apparently ideal, notably Hochob and Dzibilnocac, slinging a hammock or a tent are the only overnight possibilities. Further south some of the distances between settlements might become a little unnerving.

Hopelchen to the Edzna Ruins, 60km – The 42km ride to Cayal is not the most interesting, being a straightish road through large agricultural plantations. Taking a bus or hitching a ride to Cayal, might be a good idea, especially if it means getting to see the Edzna ruins in the cool of the morning. From Cayal, head south, the turning left is on the edge of the village. The road climbs gently over a hill, before dropping again towards Edzna. The forest comes right to the edge of this quiet road, with many butterflies and birds, making it a pleasant ride.

Edzna ruins

The ruins are impressive and free of the tourist hordes, they were restored with the help of Guatemalan refugees in the nineties. It can get very hot, so it's worth trying to enjoy the site in the cool of the morning. There's a modern visitors centre at the entrance, with a few refreshments, and nearby is a comedor.

Edzna Ruins to Campeche, 45km – Take the road west, from 1km north of the ruins, there are no places for food/drinks for another 30km. Continue for about 10km through the undulating lowland vegetation and at the first junction, take the road right. Stay on this road as it twists

and turns around the plantation fields and hacienda boundaries. After another 20km is a
marked fork to the left, this road continues into the small town of China and onto Campeche.

Campeche
This is a clean, pretty town, without the hustle and bustle of Merida. It was the main port of the
region in colonial times, and regularly attacked by pirates, hence the wall. The (imitation)
cobbled streets are laid out in the traditional grid system, and the colonial style buildings create
a very pleasant atmosphere. There are some good food markets and surprisingly few visitors to
this town. The tourist information office is just back from the seafront, at the south end of the
city wall. For places to stay, there are a couple of hostels, a trailer park, and a mix of hotels in
the town centre.

Campeche to Palenque, Chiapas, 360km – The easiest way is an overnight bus, as most of
the areas in between are uninteresting and extremely hot. Cycling south along the coast
toward Champoton, and taking a bus from there could be another option, but only for those
with plenty of time to spare. ☞ see p.36 for Chiapas

Cancun–Chetumal
Cancun to Playa del Carmen, 70km – There's a wide 4-lane highway to service the growing
number of tourist resorts on this coast. It undulates gently, has no shade and can be quite
busy, but there's plenty of room for cycling. Unfortunately there no views of the gorgeous
coastline to be had, and once past the airport junction, there are only limited opportunities for
refreshments. As a stop off, **Puerto Morales** has been recommended and is a small but
growing resort town at the half-way mark.

Playa Carmen
A popular resort for package holiday makers with plenty to do, and a little more charm than
Cancun. It's popular with the spring break crowd, and has plenty of bars, restaurants and clubs,
around a central pedestrianized area.
   There is a wide mix of accommodation from hostels to expensive hotels, with all the
normal facilities of a town like banks, internet supermarkets etc.

Playa del Carmen to Tulum, 65km – The wide road continues south, however on this section
are numerous tourist attractions; Cenotes, resorts, minor ruins, lagoons, and many
opportunities for refreshment. Views of the beaches are limited as the road is a few hundred
metres back from the coast, partly because of the large resorts, partly hurricane protection.
Though it's still possible at a few places to follow tracks to quiet stretches of beach. On
approaching Tulum the famous ruins are on the left a couple of km north of the town.

Tulum
This is a travellers/tourist hotspot for this part of the world, and an excellent place for meeting
people, or just spending a few days of complete relaxation.
The ruins, are in the most incredible position on small cliffs above the turquoise Caribbean sea.
The nearby beaches are fabulous, and stretch up and down the coast.
   At the entrance to the ruins is a small turning right that is barred to cars, it's a short cut to
and from the beaches and places to stay. Most of the accommodation is on the coast and
ranges from campgrounds and beach huts to hotels, stretching from the ruins toward the Sian
Kaan national park entrance.

The town of Tulum with banks, shops, markets and bus links straddles the highway, 3km south of the ruins. At the cross roads, just north of town is a junction with the turnings to the beaches/Punta Allen, and the road west to the Coba ruins.

Tulum to Coba ruins, 90km round trip – A visit to these ruins is well worthwhile and a bit different, because they are still partially covered in jungle. However there are trails and the main pyramids and some of the other buildings have been partially uncovered, so they can be climbed, with excellent views. For an overnight stop, camping or renting a cheap room is possible in the village, or for time out of the saddle, it's a nice day trip by bus.

There are limited opportunities for refreshments on this road and there will probably be a head wind on the way back, which may make it a nicer one way ride, with a bus back.

Tulum to Punta Allen, 60km – At present the paved surface gives way to a sandy dirt road after a few km, although there are plans to improve it in the near future.

This is a beautiful ride and there are few cars (maybe more if road is improved), most of the journey is within the **Sian Kaan national park**, and the entrance is about 15km south of Tulum. If intending to continue on the adventurous route to Sta Philippe Carillo (see below), ask the warden for any latest information or advice. There is a free campground a few km south of the park entrance (no water).

The coastal scenery is stunning, with lookout points to the lagoons inland and along the sandy beaches out to the turquoise sea. Palms and other lush vegetation hang over the road. *NB Take enough water and supplies to get to Punta Allen, as there are no shops inbetween.*

Punta Allen – Is a small fishing village and not a tourist attraction in itself, although there's a few cheap fish restaurants, and a places offering rooms. A short trip down the tracks to the lighthouse at the very end of the peninsular is easy enough, if open, it offers great views of the surrounding area.

Punta Allen to Felipe Carrillo Puerto through the Sian Kaan NP 70km – The first part is probably the most difficult, haggling with the fishermen for a lift over to the other side of the lagoon! It's only a 5 minute launch ride, but there is no other transport, try to keep it under US$10 for the sake of future travellers.

The first part of this route is not marked on the ITMB map, a track starts just over the lagoon, from Punta Allen and joins the marked track a few km from Vigia Chico
The dirt road is in reasonable condition and starts from the waters edge in lowland scrub, it then enters the low canopy forest after a couple of km, it's difficult to get lost as this old

military road is very straight.

A side trip to the fishing village of Vigia Chico is an unresearched possibility.

To spend a night in the jungle makes it an incredible experience, there's a wooden watchtower half way along the track. It's about 20m high and has space at the top to camp, this is an unforgettable experience with the views, fireflies, and sounds of animals and birds in the forest below.

The dirt road is in reasonable condition and flat. Allow at least 6 hours for cycling, this route is mostly in shade, but carry at least 4 litres of water per person and food, aim to be self-sufficient as very few cars go to and from the small fishing village of Vigia Chico. There are occasional security barriers, these are to restrict car access, and are easy to go round or under. Nearer Felipe Carillllo Puerto the forest starts to thin from local logging, and the track begins to undulate and deteriorate with the extra traffic.

NB The reverse of this route is untried, it may be possible to get a launch ride from Vigla Chico to Punta Allen, but it would be expensive. The alternative is to get to the end of the track opposite Punta Allen and wave like hell for a passing fishing boat to come and get you, this is taking quite a chance!

Tulum to Felipe Carrillo Puerto direct, 96km – The road after Tulum narrows but has long straight sections and is virtually flat. The low canopy forest lines almost the entire route and will offer some shade up to mid morning and in the later afternoon. There are only a couple of settlements with simple shops, so take enough supplies and water for the whole trip. If time is short this section is worthing taking a bus through.

Felipe Carillo Puerto – This is a useful place to have a break, and has a good market for food and supplies, but the sleepy town has little else to offer. There are regular buses in all directions from the terminal close to the plaza. The route westwards to Peto is unresearched, but could be worth exploring if wanting to go to visit the Puuc route and continue south from there.

Taking a bus to Bacalar or Chetumal are reasonable options, if wanting to avoid the long empty stretches of road.

Felipe Carrillo Puerto to Bacalar, 114km – The road continues south, with many long straight sections, the forest canopy still providing some shade except around the midday hours. Again there are only a few small roadside settlements, so travel with enough supplies. A few km after passing the junction for Majahual, views of the lake will give more scenic variety, and the forest starts to open out into agricultural land. In the more exposed areas the SE wind may be more noticeable, hopefully only as a side wind.

35

Bacalar, Lake of Seven Colours and cenote Azul
Bacalar and the surrounding area, with it's beautiful lake of seven colours, are well worth stopping for, even resting up a couple of days. There are a few hotels in and around Bacalar and more places are springing up. The deep cenote Azul is a few km further south and a beautiful place to swim. There is restaurant by the cenote, and a basic campground 1 km further south on the Chetumal road. This area can become busy at weekends with holidaymakers from Chetumal.

Bacalar to Chetumal, 38km – This last section of road to Chetumal passes through forest, it can be busy, and is currently being widened. When turning onto the east/west highway, there is normally a headwind.

Chetumal
This functional town is a popular shopping destination, and has a good interactive museum of Mayan history for tourists. The youth hostel is 5 minutes east from the centre and a cheap place to wash off the dust. There are several hotel options in the town centre. The bus station for long distance Mexican destinations, Belize or Guatemala is ten minutes north of the town centre by bike.

Chetumal to the Belize border, 13km – This is straight forward enough, and cycling can be easier than bussing because of the queues to and from the new duty free market on the border. Follow signs west out of Chetumal and after 10km, bear left; the border is another couple of km. The Mexican immigration is easy enough, however on the Belizean side, you may need to wheel your bike through the customs hall. Depending on how good it looks, the officials may stamp or write a comment in your passport, to ensure it isn't sold within Belize. ☞ see p.45 for **Belize**

Chetumal to Palenque (Chiapas), 470km – This route carries a definite recommendation for taking a bus, with perhaps with a stop-off to explore some of the ruins in the Calakmul biosphere reserve. Otherwise the distance, monotony, and heat make this a potential 3 or 4 day ordeal of endurance, rather than enjoyment.

Chiapas

This region of Mexico is very rich culturally and incredibly biologically diverse, having several different ecosystems and Mexicos only cloud forest. The climate varies from tropically sweaty in the forests and plains around Palenque to cooler and more temperate in the pine covered highlands around San Cristobal. The markets are a riot of colour as the people in traditional costume from different communities mix and trade.

It's impossible to ignore recent history, and many of the reasons that led to the Zapatista (EZLN) uprising of 1994, are still relevant today. There are some communities that openly support the EZLN, and black signs proclaiming autonomy can be seen on the roadside, don't worry they are not bandits! The overall situation is more peaceful now, though there are still many unresolved issues in the region.

Some older Mayan people don't know any Spanish, and some choose not to speak it, so it's worth learning a few words of the local languages. Genuine interest in their culture will be appreciated.

Cycling highlights
- The climb to the top of the Tzontehuitz mountain from San Cristobal is an incredible ride, with beautiful views and all kinds of interesting route variations to be explored.
- The Palenque to Occosingo road is beautiful ride through the mountains and forest.
- Any of the long descents from San Cristobal toward Occosingo, Chiapa de Corzo, or Comitan are quite a buzz, with beautiful changing scenery and excellent views.

Palenque

The town is not that exciting, but it does have some good markets, as well as banks, shops, internet and tourist info. It's also a good place to bump into fellow travellers.

The bus offices are clustered together on the road into town, for covering the long distances to Chetumal or Campeche. In town there are a wide range of accommodations to suit most budgets, and a few campgrounds on the 8km road to the ruins, most have hammock spaces, cabanas and rooms for rent as well, El Panchen after 4km is the most note worthy.

The junction for the road to the ruins is 1km out of town on the route toward Occosingo. It undulates and climbs over a couple of small hills, at the end there's a steeper climb up to the ruins entrance.

The **Palenque ruins** are real treat and their position affords great views over the plains below. For the more adventurous, there are some nice footpaths up into the forested hills, and to unexcavated ruins, right of road as it climbs to the main entrance.
There is also a museum on the right, before the road starts climbing up to the ruins entrance.

Palenque to Guatemala – The route to Frontera Echevarria gives the opportunity to visit the ruins of Bonampak and Yaxchilan, however, the distances are long and there is little inbetween the small villages en route. The short boat ride to Co-op Bethel in Guetmala will probably be double the normal price with a bicycle.

There are other routes to Peten in Guatemala, but they involve much longer boat rides, potentially difficult with a bike.

Palenque-San Cristobal

Palenque to Agua Azul, 65km – It's worth starting early as most of this journey is through hot flattish ranchland, with little respite from the sun. The couple of climbs out of the plains have a little more tree cover for shade. There are occasional roadside shops.
NB This paved road can be particularly slippery after rain.

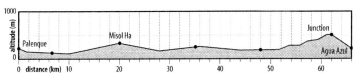

A great stop off after 20km, are the **Misol Ha waterfalls** and swimming hole. They are quite touristy, but beautiful enough to make the effort. There are refreshments and food available. Agua Azul is another 45km, the steady climb up to the junction gives some good views. The last 5km are beautiful, winding downhill through the forest.

Agua Azul

The rapids and the amazing blue colour of the water make this exciting place to swim and explore. There is a small tourist fee payable at the entrance to the village. It's a well frequented backpackers hangout if wanting to meet fellow travellers and kick back for a while. There are several different places to stay, with cabanas to rent and camping is also possible. Trails extending up and down the river for several km are worth exploring, as some of the rapids are spectacular.

NB The river whilst impressive at any time, loses it's famous blue colour after rainfall, and it can take several days to clear again. Camping out is not a good idea as there have been continual problems of theft and robbery in this area, check on the situation locally.

Agua Azul to Occosingo, 55km – The 5km steep climb back to the main road is obviously best done early. There is much more significant climbing on this route, and with the heat it can be hard work. However the route passes through some incredibly beautiful scenery, and the forest in places will give some shade.

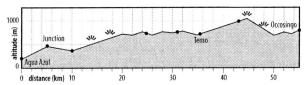

There are several small settlements enroute with roadside shops, to buy supplies or water. Nearer Occosingo about halfway up the climb from Temo, there are a few restaurants around a truck stop and at the top is a basic comedor with a look out over the Occosingo valley below

Occosingo

The town, although lacking the colonial glamour of San Cristobal, has a lively market and is the functional trading centre for a large rural area. It's a good place to experience the local culture, without the touristy knick knacks. For accommodation there are a couple of places to stay.

There is a small EZLN community, just out of town on the road to Palenque, with a variety of interesting murals and signs.

SIDE TRIP

Tonina ruins – The site is 12km through the hot agricultural plains to the east of Occosingo. The road passes a large military base, but is mainly through ranchland. There is a short climb up to the ruins site, on the north side of the valley. Although the ruins don't compare to those of Palenque in terms of size or grandeur, the peace from the lack of tourists is wonderful and there are also good views across the valley.

Occosingo to San Cristobal de las Casas, 82km – This is a hard days ride, although by no means impossible, as the gradients are all reasonable. The steepest part is the initial climb out of Occosingo, although haze permitting, this is rewarded with fantastic views back over the valley below. The beautiful scenery is of mixed forest, with good views down side valleys and into the mountains. There are occasional roadside comedors and shops, although some stretches of the road can seem remote, as the traffic is light.

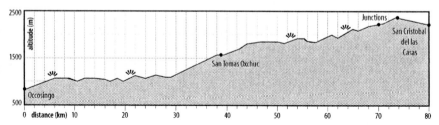

After 40km, **Sto Tomas Oxchuc** is the largest settlement on this route, where there are a couple of basic accommodations (on the road behind the municipal buildings) if wanting to spend the night. This is a traditional place and the colours of the local weavings are spectacular.

There is an alternative route to San Cristobal that leads from the back of this town (see below).

Onwards, the road whilst climbing in 'steps,' also rises and falls over a couple of valleys, the scenery is wonderful, changing with the increasing altitude to pine forest with good views through the trees to the south of the road. There are several small, traditional settlements with shops and comedors to satisfy hunger and thirst.

The gradients are reasonable all the way up to the junction for San Cristobal, the last 7km to the town are on a busier road, but downhill all the way. The town centre is a few blocks north of the highway, take the turning right next to the bus station.

The obvious alternative on this route is to take a bus, which is a reasonable option, given the climbing involved.

Sta Tomas Oxchuc to Tenjapa and onto San Cristobal, about 80km – This route isn't the easy way to San Cristobal, but it is more of an adventure.

Take the good quality dirt road to the right at the back of the plaza, towards Cancuc, this is a pretty route along a valley. At the first junction bear left to Yochib, the right turn goes onward to Cancuc (this direction is unresearched, but some buses go there from Occosingo).

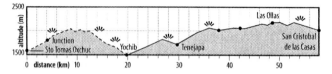

There is a significant climb with incredible views, passsing through a few coffee growing communities (basic shops) on the mountain slopes. The top is not easy to define, but after a few km the road starts a long undulating descent, which then becomes a more steady downhill. The route is steep and little more than a track in places, eventually it drops into the dusty village of Yochib, which is spread over the valley basin.

The onward route is now paved all the way to San Cristobal. There is a long, hot climb out

of Yochib with little shade, the views are the only compensation, before a descent down the side of a valley into **Tenejapa**. This is a good place for a break, particularly if there's a market on and there are basic accommodations or buses to San Cristobal if needed.

Onwards the highland scenery is mostly agricultural with patches of pine trees, there are some climbs, firstly out of Tenejapa, then up and down several side valleys. Of the settlements passed through, Las Ollas is the biggest with a couple of shops, after which there is one more valley to cross, before the long downhill into the city.

San Cristobal del las Casas

This is a delightful colonial town with a wealth of history, the markets and surrounding villages are excellent places to get to know to the local highland Mayan culture. The restaurant and bar scene is vibrant, with many internet cafes, bookshops, bike shops and other interesting and artistic ventures.

There are a wide range of accommodations from hostels to hotels, most are within 4 blocks, of the main square. The only campsite is at Rancho San Nicholas 1.5km east of town and is a peaceful place, although a good sleeping bag will be necessary for the cool nights.

The main square is a few blocks north of the main highway with the tourist information office on the east side. Map boards around the plaza now show routes into the mountains, this is a good sign of an improving situation locally, as many villages were off limits a few years ago.

This excellent design is the work of Ambar Past, you can visit her workshop called the Taller Lenateros at Flavio A. Paniagua 54 San Cristobal de las Casas

SIDE TRIPS

San Juan Chamula, 10km – This is very a much a tourist destination, although for good reason. The church and rituals associated with it are a curious mix of Catholicism and local Mayan beliefs. The church is definitely one place to leave your camera in it's bag, unsensitive tourists have in the past been assaulted for not respecting local wishes. Alcohol is an important part of the religious ceremonies, and this has led to awkward situations with tourists.

Zincanton, 26km round trip – This lovely village is much quieter than San Juan Chamula, and can easily be combined with a trip there as well. Again it's on the tourist trail, so expect plenty of shops selling merchandise. It's quite a climb back up to the Chamula junction, with little shade, before the long descent back to the City.

San Andres Larrainzer, 40km round trip – This hilltop village is a long climb from San Cristobal, but well worth the effort to experience the local culture, and the views. This village was the focus of peace talks between the Zapatistas and the government a few years ago There are regular minibuses if only wanting to enjoy the downhill on the way back.

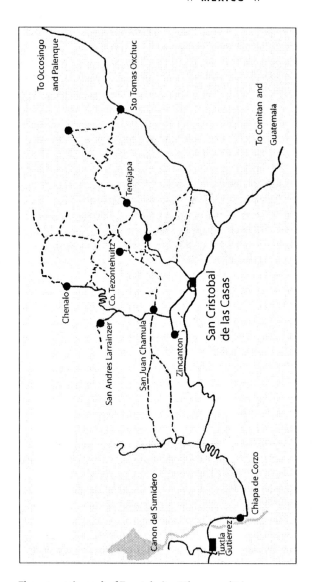

To Occosingo and Palenque

Sto Tomas Oxchuc

To Comitan and Guatemala

Tenejapa

Co. Tezontehuitz

Chenalo

San Andres Larrainzer

San Juan Chamula

Zincanton

San Cristobal de las Casas

Canon del Sumidero

Chiapa de Corzo

Tuxtla Gutierrez

41

The mountain peak of Tzontehuitz, 40km round trip.
Take the road from the main square toward the temple of Guadaloupe, this bends round the
right hand side of the church (ask for the road to Tenejapa, if unsure). Keep climbing out of
town and into the pine woodland, the road eventually bends round to the left, there are good
views to be had just off the road. Keep going through the village of Piedricitos, and in the next
couple of km, start looking out for a sign to Taza d'agua on the left. Take this track, which
winds through the forest. At the first junction bear right, following the Telmex signs. The road is
climbing all the time, but not steeply, the next junction is a four way split, bear left. It then

starts to get a little steeper, with the first signs of a settlement eventually appearing, again with great views. At the T-junction in this village turn right (left eventually leads to San Juan Chamula). The road climbs more gently, there is now more exposed rock, as the road winds around the mountain ridges. The turning up to the peak is after another few km of dips and rises and goes steeply off to the left.

The peak is 2910m, and the all round views are unforgettable. The communication masts are regularly maintained although there are some deserted buildings for shelter if the weather turns bad. Return the same way, or via San Juan Chamula.

NB Take clothes for potential cold and rain and some supplies in case the weather turns.
Be aware that much of this route is off familiar tourist paths, learning a couple of greetings in the local Mayan language will help when meeting people, some rarely if ever speak Spanish.

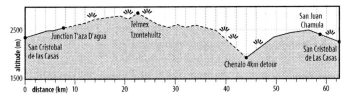

The X-section above shows a circular route from San Cristobal around the Tzontehuitz mountains.

Further exploration
NB Exploring beyond the peak will need some Spanish, a whole day and some knowledge of the current situaton in the area, it may not be so safe after dark.

From the top of Tzontehuitz, descend the short paved road and turn left, the track starts to descend and it's condition does vary. The countryside and next few villages passed through are peaceful and surrounded by small fields, please be sensitive with a camera, as these areas are completely off tourist trails. There a couple of basic shops for supplies.

Follow the road around the mountain taking the left turn at every opportunity, although check regularly by asking for directions to Chenalo, because there is one right turn after 3 or 4 junctions. Continuing there is more forest and the occasional settlements get a little larger, more run down and perhaps a little less welcoming. The road will start to descend steeply down the side of a valley, with incredible views if the clouds permit (there may be a short-cut from half-way down this descent, check locally).

The track winds down the mountainside and crosses the river, before climbing up to the paved road. Chenalo town is to the right and a couple of km further down the valley. For San Cristobal turn left, it's a long climb and about twenty km away, but the road is good condition and getting a lift shouldn't be too hard if needed.

NB Tortilla delivery in this area is done by motorbike from the tortilleria in Chenalo. At face value it seems a bizarre and funny way to progress, but in terms of halting slash and burn deforestation on the mountainsides, it makes great sense.

San Cristobal to Tenjapa (and Sto Tomas Oxchuc)
☞ see p.39 forthe description of this route in reverse and X-section

The paved route to Tenejapa is straightforward; this is a nice place to head for particularly on market days, check with the tourist office. The onward route to Sto Tomas Oxchuc should not be taken lightly, there is little shade and the climb from Yochib is particularly grueling. However it is rewarded with great views and an insight into rarely visited parts of Chiapan life.

San Cristobal to Tuxtla Guterrrez/Chiapa de Corzo and the Sumidero canyon – A side trip to the beautiful Sumidero Canyon is a nice bus journey, either both ways or just on the way back. From San Cristobal, apart from the climb out of the basin, it's mostly downhill, through beautiful mountain scenery. Starting early on the 70km ride, would make this a day to remember.

The canyon is just outside Tuxtla Gutierrez, and good value boat trips along its length are organised from Chiapa de Corzo. From Tuxtla, there's a scenic road out to the lip of the gorge, and in town there's an excellent zoo.

Tuxtla Guterriez/Chiapa de Corzo to San Cristobal, 70km – The ride is beautiful, has great views, but involves a lot of climbing, and is definitely worth starting early.

From Chiapa de Corzo, ride out across the hot plains, and get ready for the switchbacks up the mountains in front of you. After this climb it levels off for a few km , with beautiful scenery and views to enjoy. The road then starts to climb into the highlands, with the first signs of more traditional commumities and the milpa agriculture surrounding them, until the last few km when it starts to drop into the basin of San Cristobal.

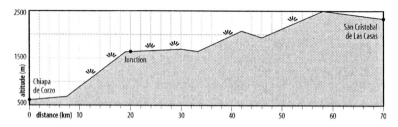

43

Alternatively, take a bus from Tuxtla, or ride to the edge of Chiapa de Corzo, buses stop opposite the gas station on the main road and are regular until it starts to get dark.

San Cristobal-Guatemalan Frontier

San Cristobal to Comitan, 85km – This is a very pleasant route on good roads. There is a 7km gentle climb up to the junction for Occosingo, the road undulates for a couple of km and then it's all down hill for 26km, the scenery is mainly forested hillsides, good views beyond, with a few settlements straggling the road. The road starts to flatten out nearer to the town of Teopisca, which has basic accommodation if needed.

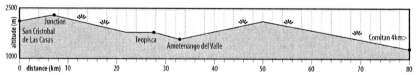

Onwards is a short descent to the junction for Las Rosas:

Turning right, this pretty route is worth considering, the ride is very pleasant passing the edge of large grassland plain, before descending through forest and ranchland. **Las Rosas** is a sizeable town and there are couple pensions/hospedajes, but no budget accommodation. *NB From Las Rosas there is quite a climb with little shade back up towards Comitan.*

Straight on the main road shortly passes Amatenango de Valle which is famous for it's home made earthenware, the only accommodation nearby is back in Teopisca. Onwards,the road starts to climb steadily, the trees change from pines to more mixed deciduous woodland, and

there are longer gaps between settlements, and very few shops. From the top of the climb there is a long descent into Comitan with some excellent views.

Comitan – The 4-lane road going through town and perhaps the bus station is all most will see of this town, but it has a little more to offer. The pleasant town centre is north of the main road, and has the necessary essentials, including accommodation if needed.

Comitan to Lagos de Montebello, 110km round trip – These lakes are well worth the side trip. Although the round trip by bike is a long one, passing through relatively flat, monotonous agricultural plains (a possible alternative are the unresearched dirt roads from the back of Comitan). This said, to visit the lakes it's probably best to stick your bike on top of a minibus. The beautiful lakes are each different shades of blue, and are easily visited by bike from the youth hostel and camping areas in the national park.

Lagos de Montebello to Nenton (Guatemala) – It is technically possible to cross into Guatemala nearby, although this border point has become a focus for illegal immigration, which may make it problematic.
    If wishing to return to Mexico in the future, getting an exit stamp is important, it may be worth checking this through with the authorities in Comitan.

Comitan-Ciudad Cuauhtemoc and La Mesilla (Guatemalan frontier), 78km – This route gets increasingly hotter with the descent into the valley basin, but has some beautiful scenery on the downhill and it gets interesting again nearer the border.
    From Comitan the straight road becomes unfeasibly wide, has no shade and undulates annoyingly! It narrows again after the junction for the airport. The turning for Lagos de Montebello comes shortly after. There are a few settlements on this hot road, though not much in between for supplies and water. The dry land vegetation is quite beautiful and the descent into the arid plains after La Trinitaria is a good buzz, although it comes with a temperature rise. Once past San Gregorio Chamic, the road starts to climb gently, although through several smaller ups and downs. The views of the massive Cuchumatanes mountains looming in the distance are awe-inspiring.
    As the road winds toward the junction for Ciudad Cuauhtemoc, it gets steeper, before levelling out on the final 2 or 3km. Clear immigration, the formalities are simple, and find some energy for the stiff but beautiful 5km climb up to the Guatemalan border

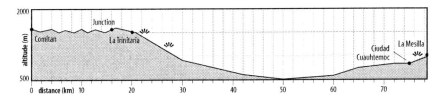

Cycling from Comitan to Huehuetenango is a long days ride, so there are a couple of options: Bus to the border and cycle from there, as the Guatemalan side is a particularly beautiful ride, or stop the night in chaotic La Mesilla where there are a couple of hospedajaes.

BELIZE

NB If planning to only transit the country quickly, there are good quality buses running from Chetumal direct to Flores in Guatemala.

Immigration – Entry for Australasians, North Americans and members of the EC is straight forward. Be prepared for the possibility of having to prove a certain degree of wealth, depending on how many days you want to stay. If your bike looks particularly good, a written reference of it may be made in your passport, this is to prevent you selling it. There are significant Conservation (departure) taxes of US$20 when leaving the country, and these are likely to increase with time.

The People – Creoles, Garifunas, different Mayan groups, Latinos, and increasing numbers from the Orient make an interesting mix of cultures. Although there seems to be little racial integration.

Language – English is spoken everywhere, although sometimes in a dialect that's difficult to understand. In parts of the south there are some latin and Mayan communities where Spanish is used.

Money and costs – Belize dollars are interchangeable at a 2:1 rate with US dollars. This in practice means that US currency is also widely accepted in shops. The cost of living is at least 50% more than the surrounding Latin countries.

45

Roads – The main highway network between towns is now completely paved, and in reasonable condition. Dirt roads are generally well compacted and maintained, although not without a few potholes

Alternative transport – Old American school buses ply most of the routes in the country, mixed with some more luxurious buses. They don't have roof racks although will normally be able to find room for a bike or two.

Cycling highlights
- The paved road from Belmopan to Dangriga (the Hummingbird highway) has beautiful scenery, with several excellent stop-offs.
- The off-road cycling into the mountains south of San Ignacio is superb.

Example of 2 week route around Belize city
Belize City-San Ignacio-Flores andTikal-Poptun- (Optional Semuc Champey-Coban-El Estor)-Rio Dulce-Livingstone-boat-Puerto Barrios-boat-Punta Gorda-Dangriga-Belize City

General tips and observations
- Belize is definitely aiming for tourists with more to spend than the average backpacker, the prices reflect this, although on a bike it's still possible to travel cheaply.
- Distances are measured in miles on signposts, and within the text of this section of the guide.
- Belize City has a bad reputation for crime, it's probably best not to explore at night, until more confident with the local culture.

Mexican frontier (Santa Elena) to Orangewalk, 39 miles – The road is wide, flat and in relatively good condition. The joke is that it was made this way so the light planes collecting

the local cash crop could land on it.! The scenery is mostly agricultural with a lot of sugarcane, and some woodland, there are regular small settlements straggling the road. Whilst not the most interesting of routes, it is pleasant enough. The predominate SE wind may be an issue, as there isn't much shelter.

Corozal is the first town passed through after 10 miles, and is relaxed and peaceful. There is a market and a few stalls selling drinks and food, along with a few places to stay if needing to spend the night. The seafront is pleasant, although there are no beaches. Onwards the scenery is much the same, although there a few more settlements along the roadside, after 7 miles is a junction:

Right – is the main paved road and a slightly longer route.

Straight on – is quieter, but becomes a dirt track for a few miles, passing through the cane fields.

The roads rejoin after 10 miles, and continue through the gently undulating countryside to Orangewalk.

Orange walk

The town has a nice atmosphere, and many surviving old wooden buildings, there is a shady plaza and covered markets, with good food stalls nearby. Other necessities include a supermarket, banking and internet facilities. For accommodation there are several guesthouses if needing to stay overnight.

Orangewalk to Belize City, 50miles – a few miles south of Orangewalk, there's a bridge over the Vew river and nearby are several companies offering tours to the Lamanai ruins, involving a launch ride along the nature rich water ways.

A little further on is a junction, the old northern highway, branches off to the left, and eventually passes close to the ruins of Altun Ha. This dirt road is badly pot-holed, which may make it perfect for slow, but traffic-free cycling.

The newer paved road continues south, and is mostly uninteresting, with the forest cleared on each side. Although after 24 miles, it passes the turning for the Crooked Tree wildlife sanctuary with it's lakes, forest tracks and bird watching.

Crooked Tree wildlife Sanctuary

The straight track to the lakes and village is about 4 miles long, the last part over a causeway seperating two large lakes. The park centre and wardens building are right on the lakeside. The wardens are helpful, and entrance fee includes a map, access to elevated walking trails and an observatory. Food, accommodation and numerous excursions are available in the surrounding spread out Crooked Tree village. The shallow lakes shrink drastically as the dry season progresses, with the best viewing in April and May, as the birds are concentrated in a smaller area. Cycling or horseback are the best ways across the lake beds to the best bird watching positions and there many excellent sandy trails to explore through the pine forest.

Continuing south to Belize City, the scenery is much the same, although there are some pretty waterways next to the road, and increasingly larger settlements as the city approaches.

Belize City
Easily explorable by bike, although be careful after dark, this town doesn't have the best of reputations. The wooden buildings do give a certain run-down charm and the mix of cultures is quite unique. The bus station is close to the markets, a few blocks from the town centre and there are all the normal facilites like tourist information, banks, internet, bike shops and a variety of accommodations (although expensive for a tight budget).

   To the islands – A bike on the larger islands like Caye Caulker or Ambergris Caye might be useful, on the smaller ones a costly pain, as shipping or flying a bike will inevitably incur a large surcharge. If planning to go it might be better to find temporary storage, bike shops in the City should be able to help.

Belize City to Belmopan, 50miles – This is a mostly flat featureless road, that once out of the city passes the zoo, then crosses the coastal plains. If it's clear, there are distant views of the Maya mountains. If deciding to take a bus, try to leave early for more time to cycle and enjoy the national parks near the Hummingbird highway.

Belmopan
This town (to be) is the Hurricane-proof Belizean capital. There are some markets near the bus station, which are useful for basic supplies. But there really is little of interest for anyone, apart from the tiny Guanacaste national park. The entrance is near the junction of the western and Hummingbird highways. There are self-guiding trails, focusing on a massive Guanacaste tree.

Belmopan to San Ignacio, 24 miles – There are views of the mountains from this road and a turning into the Mountain Pine Ridge reserve at Georgeville, a few other settlements straggle the road side, as it gradually climbs before reaching Santa Elena on the other side of the river from San Ignacio.

47

San Ignacio (aka Cayo)
This town's specialty is adventure tourism in the Maya mountains which are 11 miles south. There is a good range of accommodation, including a campsite near the river. Cayo is set in an attractive valley, and has a good atmosphere; it's a travellers place to rest up, with some nice cafes and places to eat. There are all the useful essential facilities, banks, internet etc and good up-to-date info available from tour operators and the information centre, near the market.

   There are cycling tours available from town, giving a chance to explore the far reaches the Mountain pine ridge reserve with a group.

SIDE TRIPS
There are many different companies offering exciting caving and other excursions. There is a lot of competition to choose from. Most have trips into the Mountain Pine Ridge reserve, to the caves, waterfalls or further south to the ruins of Caracol, they usually run in SUVs or vans with roofracks, excellent for stashing a bike on, if wanting to enjoy the downhills back from the mountains at leisure.

Mountain Pine Ridge forest reserve
NB Unfortunatley much of the pine forest has been sadly denuded by a pine bug. It is starting to recover, naturally and through replanting, but it will take a long time. This means there are a lack of trees giving shade, which on a hot day can make cycling hard work. On the positive side, this has given a chance for the luscious ferns and forest floor plants to prosper.
The cycling in this national park is excellent, on good quality tracks. Access is easiest by the

forested dirt road to Cristo Rey, the turning is a mile east of the main bridge in Santa Elena. Or take the bus to San Antonio and start from there.

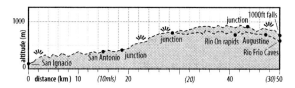

There is a network of well marked tracks and trails through the grassland and pine forest. The 30 mile ride to **Hidden falls** is excellent and the forest around them remains intact and beautiful. However the much of the forest on the way there is denuded and doing a circular ride is difficult. There is very little traffic, so getting a lift one-way with a tour company might be a good idea.

The **Rio Frio caves** are also worth a visit, although take a torch if travelling independently. The rough road from the Douglas da Silva(Augustine) forest station (shop), descends into mixed forest for 3 miles, it's then a short walk. This impressive cave is open at both ends with the river flowing through, there are also nearby walking trails to explore. It's possible to camp nearby.

There is little traffic on the road to Douglas Silva at present, although a projected new hydroelectric facility further south will lead to more heavy vehicle traffic.

Cycling to the **Caracol ruins** would be easier if a lift one-way can be arranged with one of the tour operators.

48

San Ignacio to Melchor Mencos (Guatemalan border), 11 miles – There is a steady climb, with a few smaller hills on this road. It's pretty along side the river before Benque Viejo del Carmen, which is good for swimming as well. The scenery is mostly farmland and scrub vegetation offering little shade. The nearby **Xunantunich ruins** can be visited by taking the ferry across the river and walking/cycling up the hill on the other side , although recently there has been a wave of robberies on tourists visiting this site.

From Benque Viejo del Carmen there's a small undulating climb up to the international frontier. The border isn't very exciting, although the Belizeans have built a new customs hall, which they aren't keen to allow to be dirtied by muddy bikes.

NB Keep $20 US for the Conservation (departure) tax.

☞ see p.78 for **Melchor Mencos and Peten**

Belmopan to Dangriga, 55miles (The Hummingbird highway) – This wide, paved road snakes around the foothills of the forested Maya mountains, where there is some shade from the forest on the roadside, either side of midday hours.
There are two notable highlights,

The Five Blues lakes NP – After 10 miles, there's a turning left to Saint Margaret, the small National park is nearby. There are trails and a cave to explore.

The Blue hole NP – The visitor's centre is on the edge of the road after 12 miles and has plenty of information and helpful wardens. There's a large cave system, which can be explored with a torch, walking trails and a look out tower with good views of the surrounding area. The entrance fee covers all the above, camping has been possible in the past, although there were problems with security. The Blue Hole itself is lovely place to swim, and one mile further down the road from the visitors centre.

NB Some of the trails are not well maintained, which can lead to worrying moments of feeling a bit lost. As always 'don't panic' get some bearings and retrace steps to the last marker

There are several steepish hills on this road, but the scenery will make the effort worthwhile. For provisions it's best to stock up in Belmopan, as the shops along the way are tiny and there are only a couple of cheap eating-houses and fruit stalls. One place worth stopping at about the half-way mark is Palacios mountain retreat, it's a pleasant place to camp, hitch a hammock or stay in a cabana. Augustus Palacio himself is a drum maker, and knowledgable on local herbal medicine. There is food available if just wanting a lunch break.

As the road descends toward Dangriga, the scenery becomes a little more monotonous, as citrus and other fruit plantations stretch out on both sides of the road.

The turning south toward Mayavillage and Punta Gorda is a 5 miles outside Dangriga, which is reputed to be a pleasant Garifuna town, with a few places to stay.

49

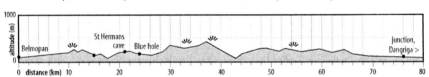

Dangriga to Mayacentre village, 22 miles – This road is now paved, so it's an easy ride across the coastal plains, with some gentle undulation, and little in the way of shade. There are several villages to pass through and junctions to Garifuna communities on the coast.

Mayacentre village aka Kendal – This new settlement is on the main road, at the junction to the reserve and has a couple of basic accommodations. It's also possible to camp in the grounds of the guest house.

Cockscomb Basin wildlife reserve
It's a pleasant 6 mile ride through the forest to the reserve entrance, where the helpful wardens have a small visitors centre. There are several walking trails, from half an hour to several hours through the forest, and some beautiful waterfalls and lookouts. Needless to say, the chances of seeing the large cats are small. It is also possible to camp on the edge of the reserve, speak with the wardens.

Mayacentre village to Placencia, 35 miles – 10 miles down the road toward Punta Gorda, there's a turning right toward Riverdale. The road down the peninsular, can apparently be in a

poor condition, although this might make it perfect for cycling slowly, perhaps with reduced tyre pressure to deal with occasional sand.

The other way to get there is by ferry from Big Creek, which is 25 miles south on the main road to Punta Gorda, then another 5miles to the coast.

Placencia – an idylic Caribbean village with good beaches and some resorts (it's being quickly developed). It hasn't been researched, but most who have been say to go soon, before it changes irrevocably. There are range of accommodations for most budgets.

Mayavillage centre to Punta Gorda, 90 miles – The road is not hugely interesting, mainly newly regenerating forest and logging camps. However it is flat until Medina bank, and even then, the hills and undulations are small.

Between Hells gate and Big fall, the scenery becomes more interesting; there are ruins worth visiting at Nim Li Punit and some nice villages. If wanting a good compromise, bussing to Hells gate, and cycling from there would work well.

Punta Gorda

Known locally as PG, this is a relaxed old town, although probably only worth an overnight stop. There are several accommodations and restaurants, with good views along the coast.

With time, the unresearched tracks into the hills around villages of Toledo could be interesting. From the main highway it's a 7 mile climb to San Antonio, which would make a good base for exploration.

Punta Gorda to Puerto Barrios (Guatemala)

The customs and immigration office is just above the quayside.

NB Keep 20$ US for the Conservation (departure) tax, this will no doubt increase regularly over the next few years

The crossing by launch can be bruising but fun if the wind is up and it takes about an hour There's an unfixed excess fare for bicycles and it's worth turning up early to ensure there's enough room.

☞ see p.91 for **Puerto Barrios and Guatemala**

GUATEMALA

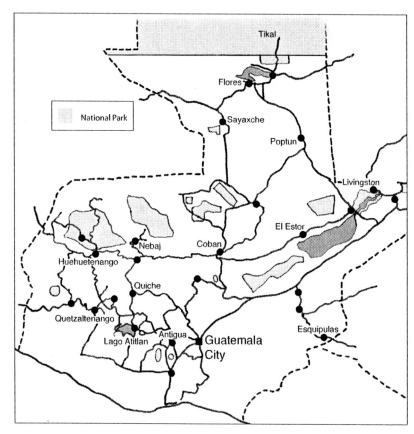

Immigration – Entry is straight forward enough for Australasians, North Americans and members of the EC, although the entrance tax can vary. 90 days is the usual amount given. Recently the authorities have started to require visitors to fill out a simple tourist card, it needs to be kept safe andhanded over to immigration on departure

The people – This is a densely populated country, and the mix of peoples is unique in Central America. Mayans, who come from several different groups, make up half the population, with mixed Latin and Mayan (Mestizos) almost the other half. There are a few communities of black Garifunas on the Caribbean coast, and a small but increasing population of expatriates.

Money – The Quetzal, a bird whose long green tail feathers were highly prized by the ancient Maya, is also the unit of currrency.

Language – Spanish is spoken throughout the country, along with several regional Mayan tongues. It's a good place to practice Spanish as for half the population it's a second language and so spoken in a simpler form, this makes it easier for Spanish novices to gain confidence in conversing.

Roads – The road network is rapidly being paved or improved, and this will no doubt continue. However maintenance of existing roads is sometimes not as good and newly paved dirt roads are often only given an inch of asphalt, which doesn't last for long, and leads to large pot holes. At the moment, it is still possible to traverse most of the country on dirt roads and tracks.

The main roads are generally quiet on Sundays, although the highway to the Caribbean coast from the Capital is not recommended at any time.

Alternative transport – The Old American school buses, painted in an all manner of colours have become a national symbol. They are ideal for transporting anything from chickens to bicycles, due the big racks on the roof.

Fares are cheap, although there are varying extra charges for carrying bikes. The conductors will sometimes try to ask for an extra fare for transporting a bike. Offering to pay half extra is reasonable, especially if he's put the bike on top of the bus. The exception to this are routes around the Capital or Antigua, where paying double is normal.

The seat space is predictably tiny, long legged people will need to opt for the aisle seat, but on some routes it's not unusual to have the aisles completely full as well. It's not unusual to meet some interesting people, and have a laugh on board.

NB. If everyone standing starts to duck, it's probably passing a police check-point, overcrowding gets the owner a fine. The driver will thank everyone if he gets away with it!

Pick-ups in the more rural areas are taxis and general transport. The prices are comparable to the bus fares, and it would be normal to charge more for a bike. It's quite impressive how many people can fit in!

The countryside – For such a small country, the variety of landscapes is incredible. There is thick jungle and ranchland in Peten. In the highlands, many areas are covered in patchwork agriculture, some with thick rain forest or differing pine species. In the centre of the country the areas of semi-desert, with cactus and other dryland plants. On the Pacific coast agriculture dominates, from ranches to fruit and coffee plantations higher up the volcanoes. In addition there are beautiful lakes, beaches and wetlands.

General tips and observations
- Many travellers refer to Guatemala as a busy country, and it's growing rapidly in many ways.
- Market days are the best times to see small highland towns at their brightest and most interesting, especially in areas where traditional costumes are still worn.
- It's distressing in a country with a reputation of producing excellent coffee, that often in the markets and many restaurants the only coffee available is instant granules. For the 'real' thing cafes in Antigua, Quetzaltanango or other major towns are the best bet.
- Place names are often a mix of old Mayan and Spanish words, although usually only one half of the name is used, depending who you speak to.
- It's well worth the smiles in trying to learn a few words of the local Mayan languages.
- Guatemala has numerous language schools, and is a cheap place to learn Spanish. The main centres being Quetzaltenengo, Lago Atitlan and Antigua.

Cycling highlights
- Huehuetenango to Todos Santos and onto San Antonio Huista.
- Huehuetenango to Sacapulus and on toward Coban.
- Antigua to Lago Atitlan.

• Coban to Fray Bartoleme de las Casas.
• Coban to Teleman and Senahu.
2 week route around Guatemala City
Guatemalacity-Antigua (+side trips)-Lago Atitlan (side trip to Chichistenango)-Quetzaltenango (+side trips)-Huehuetenango-Ixil Triangle-Coban-Guatemala City.

The western highlands

La Mesilla to Huhuetenango, 80 km – This is a wonderful ride with great scenery and generally quiet roads. On the down side, it will be an introduction to the infamous bus drivers, they're not that bad, but be aware! The paved road climbs out of La Mesilla, and then decends, crossing a valley to Camoja Grande, which is a pleasant place to stop for food and supplies. The road at this junction heads off toward Nenton and Jacatenango.

There's another hill into the next valley, before the road climbs steadily beside the Rio Selegua. The mountains loom on both sides, much of these highlands are agricultural, with maize planted on impossibly steep slopes. This valley becomes steadily narrower and more impressive, the gorge section further up is particularly beautiful.

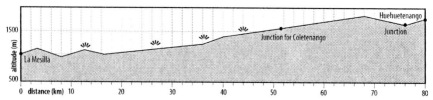

From the top of the valley there's a descent to the junction for Huehuetenango and then a 5km gentle climb up to the town.

There are several villages, and many small settlements along the way with a couple of side trip possibilities:
Colotenango – after 52km is a 3km, steep climb out of the valley to the right. This traditional settlement, has good views and there are places for food.
San Juan Atilan – is reachable from the road, although will involve some serious climbing or a pick-up ride, this route is unresearched. The other way to visit this village is the beautiful walk over the mountains from Todos Santos. It's always worth aiming for the market days on Thursdays and Sundays if possible.

Huehuetenango to La Mesilla – Being predominately downhill, makes it a very pleasant journey. It's worth considering getting to the border with enough time to cycle to Comitan or for a bus toward San Cristobal. Climbing out of the hot plains on the Mexican side would be hard work, and there is very limited accommodation until Comitan.

Huehuetenango
A prosperous large town, the new bus terminal is a 3 km from the centre just off the road to the to the highway and much of the market trade has gradually moved to surround it, with a lively mix of locals and people from the surrounding mountains coming to sell their produce.

There is a good mix of hotels in the town centre, more comfort by the main square, and the very cheap lodgings near the old market, 2 blocks behind. New cafes, internet facilities and restaurants are cropping up all the time.

The nearby **Zacleu ruins**, are a bad example of early restoration efforts, being concrete clad and not pretty. But if wanting an excuse for a short ride, head west from the plaza out of town for the 9km round trip.

Huehuetenango to Quetzaltenango (Xela), 69km – At present, much of this main road is in a poor condition, although it is being improved slowly. So unless it has had some prolonged work (widened and resurfaced), then it's worth taking the bus (there are good views through the trees to the left).

If wanting to cycle, try to plan for a Sunday, when at least there is a lot less traffic. The road crosses several valleys, before climbing over the highlands, there are only a few settlements on the way, so bring enough food.

After 58km there's a possible side trip to the market town of **San Francisco el Alto**. This is a short steep climb from the main road, and worth it for the good views from the plaza, and the big friday market. Further along this road is **Momostenango**. (☞ see p.64)

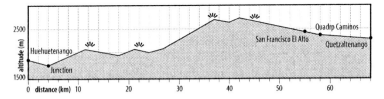

The main road continues to the busy junction of Cuatro Caminos, turn right and enjoy the flat ride across the plains to **Quetzaltenango**.(☞ see p.63)

The Cuchmatane Mountains

The highlands above Huehuetenango are beautiful, but in a stark way. The plains are mainly grass, with a few hardy cactus, loose stone walls, rocky outcrops and stunted trees. Highland life can be harsh, the thin earth of these mountains is not the volcanic rich soil of other areas, and for many it's enough to eek out a living, these are hardy peoples. There are incredible views to be had, but they are sometimes obscured by clouds or mist. Market days are worth aiming for to see towns at their most lively and interesting.

The route to San Mateo Ixtatan and Barillas takes several hours by bus as there are many long climbs, although the road is now paved as far as Soloma, in some places it seems to cling to the mountainside.

Michael Shawcross, with many years experience in the area has recommended the routes to San Miguel (it may be necessary to come back the same way) and San Rafael, although they haven't been cycled. Exploring in this direction will surprise locals, who rarely see tourists, even on the buses. There is basic accommodation in all three of the above towns.

From Barrilias, there is an uexplored 2 day route through the mountains to Chajul in the Ixil triangle. The first part has a slippery rocky suface, after rain it's treacherous, and one of the few challenges the author declined!

Huehuetenango to Todos Santos, 40km – Once through Chiantla the dirt road starts to climb steeply, and there is no let up for the next 15km, with little shade and few places to stop for refreshment.

NB If planning only to visit Todos Santos in the mountains, it may be worth leaving your bike behind. Firstly because of the tough 1000+m climb, though mainly because there are some excellent walks out of Todos Santos. Another option is to take the bus to the lookout(mirador) at the top of the climb and cycle from there.

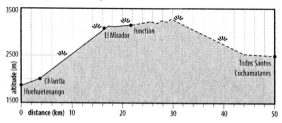

Near the top, on a clear day, the views are incredible from the lookout, and there are a few shops nearby for supplies.

The ride across the highland grassy plains is relatively easy, unless the weather is against you, as there is little shelter. The route is paved until it branches off the Soloma road, where there are a couple of comedors. The loose gravel dirt road then climbs through a couple of traditional villages, and gives the first sights of the colourful local costumes. There are a couple of climbs with a few dips and hollows before some amazing views at the pass called El Viento. It's then a steady descent, with amazing views into the valley of Todos Santos.

NB Be aware that over exertion at these altitudes can be dangerous until fully acclimatized.

Todos Santos

The local men of this valley and are famous for being one of the few Mayan groups where the men retain their traditional dress, particularly their bright red striped trousers. Market days are less imporant than they used to be, as there is now a purpose built permanent market. However the Wednesday or Saturday markets are still worth aiming for, there are a few accommodations, although be aware that the town can be full of tourists at these times. The deep valley in which the small town nestles, has paths to explore on both sides, a longer walk to San Juan Atitan, is worth considering for it's market days on Thursday and Sunday.

As a cycling side trip, the descent to San Martin would be a nice day out, getting the bus back later on, takes the pain out of it.

Todos Santos – Jacatenango and onto La Mesilla

This is a interesting route, and gives a real insight into the local culture, with beautiful mountain scenery.

55

The ITMB map should not be relied on for navigating in this area
From Todos Santos the road drops down to cross the river, then climbs up and down the valley side, passing several traditional settlements. After several km, the route starts to descend more steadily toward San Martin(unmarked on the ITMB map).The road can be rough in places with loose stones, and would be hard work to cycle in the other direction.There are basic accommodation options in the large village of San Martin.

A couple of roads cut through from San Martin to San Antonio Huista saving some hard work, but the 11km journey to Concepcion Huista is well rewarded with incredible views.

San Martin to Concepcion Huista – There are two climbs on the dirt road to Concepcion Huista, after the first is a settlement in a small valley with a couple of shops. The second climb is particularly brutal, being steep with a lot of loose stone, however if climbed (or walked) at the end of the day the sunset views are an excellent compensation. The last few km wind through forested ridges, before dropping gently into Concepcion

There is basic accommodation in the centre of **Concepcion Huista** but it isn't advertised (ask locally), the views from this town are incredible. For food there are a couple of basic comedors at the back of the market building.

The beautiful 9km descent to Jacaltenango is rough in places, and winds down the side of the mountain through the forest, coffee and maize. The approaching town can be seen from quite high up, and on the other side of the valley is a flattened area which has some ruins.

Jacaltenenago (AKA Jaca) – is a small town, though the largest settlement for some distance. It does have a variety of food and a couple of accommodation options, with a large market running down several streets.
Onwards options:
Turning right at the bottom of town (by the gas station), there's an undulating descent direct to the Nenton road,
Or a climb over the ridge to San Antonio Huista. This is a pretty route with good views on both sides, although steep in places. Half way up, there's a sharp bend to the left, and the gradients become kinder up to the pass, where theres a shrine for travellers. The descent down the other side is steep and stony in places.
San Antonio Huista – The nicest place in the area to aim for to stop the night, although lacking the great views of towns higher up, this tidy town has a few places to stay and is a pleasant place to relax.

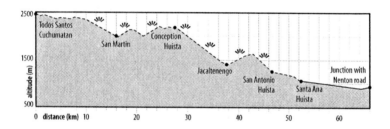

San Antonio Huista to La Mesilla – The descent continues through farmland and smaller settlements, with a steeper descent down into Santa Ana Huista, which has a small market and places to eat. Onwards the road is paved, and a nice ride undulating beside the river, there are some lovely big trees along this stretch for shade. Further down, the road climbs out of the valley, with a couple of short steep hills to the junction with the Nenton road:
Left leads toward Mesilla, and climbs and falls over a couple of valleys, before climbing steadily to Camoja Grande at the junction with the highway from Huehuetenango to La Mesilla.
The dry land scenery on this road doesn't offer much shade and there are very few places for refreshments.
Right heads to Nenton and is unresearched, theres a possible route into Mexico via the Lagos de Montbello, if planning this route check with the Mexican consul in Huehuetenango.

Huehuetenango to Sacapulus, 50km – This pleasant dirt road ride was the push to eventually write this guide, it is now gradually being paved. The scenery varies from shady pine woodland with local agriculture and a couple of rocky valleys in between, whilst there are some climbs, the gradients are all reasonable.

57

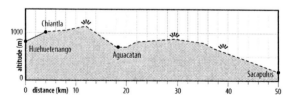

Head north out of town up to Chiantla (5km), and bear right at the first junction. The next section follows the contours of the hillside and is pleasantly shaded by pine trees. The road then climbs steadily over a ridge with good views, before descending into the town of **Aguacatan** after 18km.

This town is well worth stopping for, especially on market day, and there are some basic lodgings for staying overnight. It's a short ride to the river source, fuente San Juan, north of town. The water is freezing, but there are bathing facilities if wanting a splash.

Onwards, the road climbs steeply out of the valley and then more gently through farmland for a few km, before following a river downstream with increasing temperatures toward Sacapulus.

Sacapulas
This sleepy, hot town is at the crossroads of two cross-country routes. There are several places for food on both sides of the river, and further up into town are a few stalls under the shade of the large trees in the plaza, a nice place for a break. If needed, basic accommodation is available

close to the bridge, and there are hot(ish) springs to wallow in on the nearby river bank.
☞ see p.61 for the route towards **Sta Cruz Quiche and Chichistenango**.
If wanting to avoid the Ixil triangle, but carry onto toward Coban, the turning off the Nebaj
road is after about 5 or 6 km steady climbing and obvious as there is no other junction. This
road is level for a couple of km, then drops increasingly more steeply down toward **Cunen** for
another 5km(☞ see p.59). There are occasional pickups and buses from Sacapulus.

Sacapulus to Nebaj (Ixil triangle), 30km – There are two big ascents on this route, made
more diffficult because the road is stoney and rutted. This road seems to constantly need some
work, but as it's improved it will become easier. As ever the compensations of the climb are
incredible views.

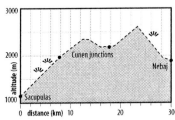

The only junction on the first climb is a turning right to Cunen. There are very few
opportunities for refreshments or water, although in the valley between the two main
climbing sections is a village with a couple of shops. The second climb, is a slightly better dirt
road, there are a few more highland small holdings and people on these slopes. The views
from the top, over the valleys below are quite special, and the descent towards Nebaj is
through a beautiful lush landscape of forest and fields.
    Alternatively, a bus to Nebaj is not a bad idea given the amount of climbing or if the
weather over the mountains is not so good. Wait on the roadside next to the market stalls, on
the other side of the bridge, as a pick-up might stop before one of the several buses comes.

The Ixil triangle
Nebaj
The green sloped mountains around Nebaj are beautiful and the expanding town, whilst
prosperous, is normally relaxed. Market days on Thursdays and Sundays bring in many people
from outlying villages, the mix of colours and patterns on the womens' costumes are quite special.
For accommodation there are a mix of basic hospedajes, and a couple of hotels as well.
*NB There is occasionally a noisy generator at night, near the base of the communications
    mast, choose your room carefully.*

SIDE TRIPS
Walking guides are available if wanting to explore the mountain sides in greater depth. One of
the nicest walks is to **Acul**. This model village was built by the military, during the civil war. It's
set in a gorgeous rolling green valley, and it's possible to buy Swiss style cheese from a farm
on the northern edge of the village. To get there, it's possible to cycle, but far more pleasant to
walk the 4 or 5km over the hills to the west of Nebaj, and drop down into the lush alpine
valley. The path is easy to pick up from town and should be safe, ask for basic directions or
organise with a local guide.

58

San Juan Cotzal, 13km and Chajul, 15km

The countryside in this direction is beautful, with patches of forest and agriculture around the settlements. The people are surprised to actually meet a foreigner, as most pass by in a cloud of dust. The ride to these other two towns has been paved for a few km, although it was a bad job, probably a grand presidential gesture! The road beyond this can be a bit rough, it undulates across valleys and then there is a 250m climb, steep and stoney in places, but there are good views from the top. The road then descends to the junction where the route divides to each of these towns:

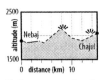

Right - goes to San Juan Cotzal.

Left - goes to **Chajul** and continues to descend for a few km, passing through a small village, and crossing a river, before starting to climb steadily up to the town. There are a couple of cheap places to stay, and it's worth doing so, even if for only one night. The church for a town of this size is incredible, and there are excellent views of the surrounding countryside.

There's an onward unresearched, but reputably beautiful, route to **Barillas** that might be possible in a day, but would be more enjoyable broken with a nights camping. This route is not to be taken lightly, the tracks nearer Barillas can be treacherous after rain, and there are a couple of small rivers to ford.

Onto **San Juan Cotzal**, descend out of Chajul and turn left at the edge of town, the route is straight forward and mostly downhill, this 6km short cut joins the Cotzal road just outside the village, it's then a short ascent to the centre. Again there are a couple of basic places to stay, though the settlement is nestled in a valley, and doesn't have the views or atmosphere of Chajul. The road back to Nebaj climbs steadily to the original junction.

Ixil Triangle–Coban

This route passes through one of the most beautiful valleys in Guatemala, although it can be demanding due to the remoteness and the state of the roads, they seem unlikely to be improved in the near future.

Nebaj to Urspantan, 42km – It's a quite a climb back over the mountain ridge, although not without the rewards of good views. In the settlement at the bottom of the descent is a junction left for Cunen, followed by another long steady drop downhill on dusty roads.

Cunen is a small, quiet place, with little to hold anyone, although it's pleasant enough for a meal break and there is a basic hospedaje if needed. It's worth stocking up on food for the next section as there are only a few small, isolated agricultural communities.

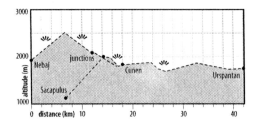

The dirt road climbs gently for a few km, before descending steeply over loose stones, around the mountainside. There's little shade but excellent views. Once round the valley head, the road

climbs steadily passing over a ridge, before descending through agricultural lands and small villages into the Urspantan valley, there's a short climb into the town. A few buses come every day from Quiche to Urspantan with occasional pickups and trucks.

Urspantan
This town is famous for being close to the family home of the Nobel Peace Prize winner, Rigoberta Menchu. It is a peaceful place, though there isn't a great deal to do apart from wander the markets. There are a couple of hospedajes, and a few comedors near the plaza.

Urspantan to Coban, 70km – The most stunning section of this route is from Chicaman to San Cristobal Verapaz, it's also the most remote. Although the distance appears manageable in a day, don't underestimate how slow going it can be. There are a few trucks and a couple of early buses to the markets in Coban, or occasional pick ups, if stuck or out of energy.

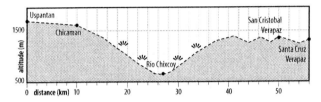

The road undulates through farmland to Chicaman, this is the last settlement of any size for 40 (slow) km. Onwards there's a brief climb, before it starts to descend, steeply in places, the surface is rough and with some loose stone. There are several more dips and rises as it passes over a ridge into the Chixoy valley. The final descent to the river is steep places, with more awkward loose stone.

There are only occasional places for food, notedly just before and at the bridge across the river. The views in this valley are incredible, and continue on the long 10km climb up the other side. The scenery is of cleared agricultural land in the valley, higher up it moves into forest and coffee plantations, there are no settlements on this section until Sta Elena. Toward San Cristobal and Santa Cruz Verapaz are many more hills, although the road surface is much better and paved from the former.

Turning left on the main road to Coban is a steady climb over a ridge through more coffee plantations, there's plenty of space for cycling on this busy road.

☞ see p.85 for Coban and routes to the Caribbean via Tactic and El Estor.
see p.88 for routes south via Rabinal to the capital.

Sacapulus-Chichistenango and onto Lago Atitlan

Sacapulus to Sta Cruz del Quiche, 45km – This is a hard climb toward the markets of Chichistenango and Lago Atitlan, although there are regular buses to Quiche and beyond if needed.

The 1000m climb up the paved road for is 20km long; the gradients are reasonable, with some dips around side valleys. There is no shade, as only sparse pine woodland dots the slopes until higher up, with some agriculture in the valleys.

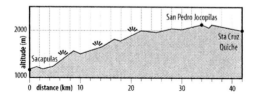

There are occasional villages, for basic food. A consolation is the temperature gradually falling with increased altitude. The road stops climbing on the last 10km to the larger settlement of San Pedro Jocopilas, although still undulates heavily. The forest thickens but still doesn't offer much shade on the road. Onwards, for the last 8km to Quiche, the road is mainly downhill.

Sta Cruz del Quiche aka Quiche

A relaxed town, it's a nice place to have a break and a bite to eat. With a bit longer the markets, which line the narrow streets behind the main church, are worth a wander.

If on a tight budget, it might be a bit cheaper than Chichistenango for accommodation. The ruins of Utatlan, 3km to the west, were once the capital for the Quiche people and could be worth a visit with time to spare. Tecum Anum, the former leader of the Quiche was honoured (?) on the now disued 0.5 Quetzal note.

Quiche to Joyabaj, Mixco Viejo ruins and onto Guatemala City or Antigua, 140km

This quiet route is completely off the tourist trail, the Mixco viejo ruins have been well restored and are worth a visit and the road has a good paved surface all the way.

The road climbs over a few pine-forested hills, with the usual mix of agriculture on the flatter sections in between. There are several larger settlements, although the one place worth having a break in is **Joyabaj** after 55km. It has basic accommodation, good markets and some interesting walks into the hills and down the cobbled road to the river. A challenging ride would be the climb over the mountains to Cubulco, this has been explored on foot but not all the way, so better to ask advice locally on track conditions.

Onwards to Mixco Viejo is an unresearched section, the route passes through Pachulum

61

where there' a junction with a new paved road (unmarked on most maps) that cuts through to the capital. It passes through the very hot Motugua valley with the restored Mixco Viejo ruins a couple of km from the river. Normally the ruins are very quiet, although at the weekends, there are a few more city folk visiting. If hoping to avoid the climb with a lift, this is the best time to go. There are a couple of buses from Pachulum to the Capital, but they leave in the morning.

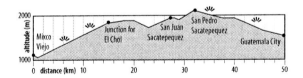

The 1200m climb out of this valley up to San Pedro Sacatepequez is long and hard because of the heat. For the first few km there are very few opportunities for refreshment and little shade, although increasingly good views behind. At the top of the first part of the climb, there are junctions to El Chol and San Raymundo. Onwards there's thicker pine forest, which gives some shade. This road can be busier at times, and starts to descend into a narrow valley, then there's a steady climb up the other side to San Juan Sacatepequez. This town has a pleasant square, and is a nice place for a break, as there's another 5km of climbing up to **San Pedro Sacatepequez.** This town has a lot of character, with a large church and markets, it's easy to lose a sense of direction, as the streets wind around the mountain slopes. There is accommodation available if needed.
The following routes are included on the large scale inset of Antigua and the Capital on the ITMB map.

From San Pedro Sacatepequez, it's downhill which ever way you go:
To **Guatemala city** it's another 20km, as the winding road descends out of the forest, and into the suburbs of the city.

To Antigua – It's a pretty ride, through rich agricultural lands to San Lucas Sacatepequez, these roads are now paved, onwards there's a fast descent down the 4-lane highway into Antigua, with excellent views.
Or another route to Antigua is via Zenacoj, and through more pine forest. There's a steep valley to negotiate after Zenacoj, before a short stretch on the Pan American highway to Sumpango. From there turn right, the last section is a descent through thick dust on the dirt roads to Jocotenango on the outskirts of Antigua.

Sta Cruz del Quiche to Chichistenango, 13km – Heading south past the large army base, the road crosses a plain before climbing gently through sparse pine forest. After a few km, there is a pretty, steep sided valley to cross, the forest becomes denser with increased altitude, and gives more shade. Continuing around the mountainside, the road drops into another valley and then climbs steadily alongside a river, before an increasingly steep ascent into town.

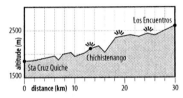

62

Chichistenango

This colourful town is perched on a hillside with excellent views over the valleys below. Heaving with tourists, it is one of the principle destinations of organised tours. The main markets are on Sundays and Thursdays and the narrow streets are teeming with merchandise and handicrafts from all over Guatemala. There are a few places to stay, and some plush hotels, although not so many budget options, the cheapest are on edge of town on the road toward Los Encuentros.

The other side to this commercial town is a strong adherence to ancient beliefs, and many locals still worship at Mayan shrines on the mountain sides.

Chichistenango to Lago Atitlan, 35km – This road can be busy with tourist buses and traders to and froing from the markets. After a short climb out of town, the road drops sharply into a beautiful, deep forested valley. The 450m climb up the other side is well graded but made harder with all the traffic. Once out of the valley, the scenery becomes more agricultural as the road undulates and climbs steadily up towards the Los Encuentros junction on the Pan-American highway.

To Solola and Panajchel, the road descends to a junction, and turning left down again onto a high agricultural plain, before dropping down towards Solola.

☞ see p.68 for **Lago Atitlan,** and p.69-72 for routes to **Antigua.**

Quetzaltenango (Aka Xela)

This town is the cool (climatically!) place to learn Spanish. Architecturally it can't compete with Antigua, but the local culture is vibrant and a little more alternative. There are many cafes to sample the excellent local coffee, and all the usual conveniences of a city.

There are several markets in different parts of the city, selling handicrafts from the entire area. The main cloth/fabric markets are on the western edge of town, the main bus terminal is nearby. Accommodations are mostly within a couple of minutes ride from the plaza.

Xela is a centre for voluntary work of all kinds, from tree planting to working with street kids. Most projects require a commitment of several weeks.

There are several good organised excursions for climbing local volcanoes, such as Santa Maria and Chicabal.

ONE-DAY ROUTES FROM QUETZALTENANGO (XELA)
Zunil and the Fuentes Georgina
These are the best hot baths in Guatemala, there is a small entrance fee, and they are open every day from 8 o'clock, with several pools to choose from. The intact forest around them is beautiful and there are footpaths to explore, of varying difficulty, to the local volcanic peaks. *NB The temperature of the water does vary from time to time.*
There are two roads to the village of Zunil, at the foot of the climb up to the hot baths:
The most direct goes south via Amolanga and involves a steepish climb, before descending toward Zunil;
The other is longer, but with easier gradients. At the fork on the western edge of town head right on the Pacific highway(left goes to Quadra Caminos). This a good quality paved road and well graded, it also saves the short climb out of Zunil.

This is an interesting village, one of a few that looks after an effigy of San Simon(Maximom). Ask locally for the current residence of this renegade saint, visiting will involve a few coins.

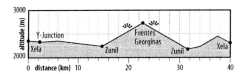

The X section above shows a circular route, using both possibilities.
The turning to the baths is marked and is above Zunil, on the Pacific highway. It's a consistent 8km climb, through farmland and forest, not too steep, and well rewarded at the end. At the junction, halfway up, bear right.

Xela to Momstenango, 27km – Momstenango is the home of the weavers who make the finest woollen clothes and blankets in Guatemala. The best days to go are Sunday and Wednesday when the market is on.

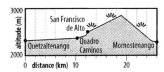

This journey is straight forward, head west to Quado Caminos and turn left, climbing for 3km on the busy Huehuetenango road. Turn right and climb steeply up into the town of **San Fransisco el Alto.** There's a big traders market on Fridays, which attracts people from all over the highlands, and good views from the plaza, across the plains below. Alternatively take a bus to San Francisco Alto, this removes the busy and uninteresting roads from the journey and leaves a beautiful ride. From San Francisco the good paved road, climbs steadily for 6km, with occasional good views, through the pine trees, before a long descent toward Momostenango.

Momstenango
This pleasant town has all the usual facilities of a prosperous market centre and a couple of attractions other than it's woollen goods.
The hot baths are a couple km descent north of town. They are communal(a bit much for some!) and can get very dirty by the end of the day. Some weird rock formations can be found nearby, although they are only worth a visit if bored or wanting to get out for a ride.
There are a few basic accommodation options, in the town centre.
Going back to Xela it maybe worth considering a bus to avoid the 700m climb, although the road is well shaded by pine forest.
It is also possible to continue from Momstenango toward Quiche or Sacapulus on reasonable dirt roads.

Xela to Totonicapan, 18km – This town can be visited most easily by following the road up the pretty river valley from Quatro Caminos, this leads all the way to this town, and whilst pleasant, it's necessary to come back the same way.
The other option is a nice round trip involving a ride or bus up to Alaska, the highest point on the Pan American highway. Turn left near the small settlement at the top, and start the long descent on the old road to Totonicapan. This road is partially paved and in a bad state of repair in places. However, there's very little traffic and good views down into the Totonicapan valley. Lower down, the mountain slopes are heavily farmed, with increasingly large settlements.

Totonicapan
This town sits in a deep valley basin surrounded by smaller settlements and a dense patchwork of fields. It's off the main tourist paths, but as a department capital it's an important trading centre, with a big twice weekly market. There is basic accommodation if required.

Xela–Ixchiguan (near Vols. Tajamulco and Tacana)
From Xela, bus or cycle to San Marcos, then climb onto the highland plains for incredible views of snow capped volcanoes to Ixchuagan. The scenery is sometimes desolate, though always beautiful. Descend back the same way, or climb to the roof of these mountains and descend through everchanging landscapes to Coletenango and back to Huehuetenango. This would make a nice 2/3 day trip.
The routes are clearly marked on the ITMB map, although there some newly cut roads as well. From Sochel, there are roads to Coletenango, ask directions regularly.
NB Due to the altitudes involved, give your body a chance to acclimatise.

Sometimes its nice to see the world from a different perspective!

65

Quetzaltenango (Xela) to San Marcos, 56km – Fortunately this highway is not the main route from Xela to the Pacific coast, although it can still be busy with local traffic, and those heading toward the border. Cycling out across the plains, there isn't much space for cyclists on the road. There are several settlements, Ostuncalco being the largest, none are particularly interesting, but good for food breaks. The climb into the pine forest, will give good views, and some shade either side of the midday hours, there are a few small agricultural communities in the mountains although it would be better to take supplies as shops will be basic. There are a few valleys to cross, before a long descent to **San Pedro Sacatpequez.**
　This is a modern large town with a few places to stay, if needing to break a journey. It's only a few km to **San Marcos**, which has an older more traditional feel to it, which also has some accommodation. Neither towns are particularly interesting from a touristic viewpoint, just good bases for further exploration.

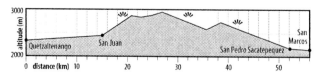

Taking a bus from Xela to San Marcos or San Pedro and cycling from there is reasonable, to avoid the highway traffic, and save energy for the bigger more interesting climbs to come.

San Marcos to Ixchiguan, 39km – The road is now paved all the way to Ixchiguan. There are only a few shops or other opportunities for refreshment. There is a long climb out of San Marcos, but the gradients are ok, and the winding road offers great views over the lands below.

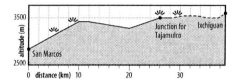

Once on the high plains, the views should be food enough to keep going. Bear left at the first junction, and prepare to start climbing again. Passing snow capped Vol. Tajamulco on the left, the road to Tajamulco town is also left at the next junction. Right/straight on is the road to Ixchiguan. At this point most of the climbing has been done, as the road levels out, although save a bit of energy for the short, steep climb into this settlement.

Taking the bus to Ixchiguan and cycling back to San Marcos, is the obvious more relaxed way of seeing these highlands.

Climbing the volcano of Tajamulco is possible from this route, although unresearched.

Ixchiguan – This simple highland village has basic accommodation and a couple of places to eat near the market place. The views are incredible; watching the clouds bubble up from the Pacific plains, around the volcanoes is particularly pleasing.

The road to Calico can be in bad condition, if considering an alternative route. Check locally, for the current state. There is a slight Wild West feel to this area, be aware that all roads near the borders are militarily sensitive.

Ixchiguan to Colotenango about 50km – This journey is a bit of an adventure, allow at least 6 hours, as the views are worth spending time to enjoy and the body is much less efficient at these altitudes. Although this route is predominately downhill, there are many small climbs on the way. Finding the right road is not always easy, because several new roads have been made recently, and there are not many people around to ask directions from, so good confident navigation skills are essential.

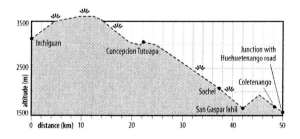

The rough track from the back of town descends briefly, and crosses a small brook. Then after climbing for a couple of km, it joins a better quality dirt road. Head right, the road is climbing though more gently, and eventually passes a large black rock on the left. Soon the road bends round to the left, on a large windswept plain, the track/path wanted veers off to the right/straight on, although will be easy to miss. Check directions with locals if possible. If it is missed, don't panic. Follow the road, it eventually starts to descend, passing through a small settlement called Santa Cruz, after a couple of km. There's a turn off to the right shortly after which climbs over several small valleys back to the same route. This road although having many turn-offs is fairly obvious and starts to flatten out into more agricultural land, before climbing over a small ridge into the town of **Concepcion Tutuapa**, there are basic hospedajes here if needed. Onwards the number of dirt roads become even more complicated, ask directions regularly, first to Sochel, then to Coloteneango. The vegetation grows lusher, a lot of coffee is grown on the steep slopes and although it is mainly downhill, sometimes very steeply, there are some climbs, notably out of the valley from the small village of San Gaspar Ixphil to **Colotenango** which has a couple of shops. It's then all downhill for the last couple of km to the highway.

☞ see p.53 for routes to Huhuetenango or the Mexican border.

Quetzaltenango (Xela) to Lago Atitlan, about 70km – This route is beautiful, but best cycled on a Sunday when the Pan American highway is quieter, also for the market in Nahuala. There are usually several other locals in lycra out for a ride as well. Take refreshments, as there are only a few shops on the climb.

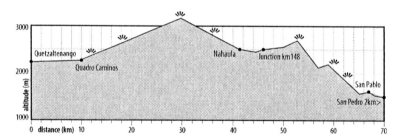

The 15km climb starts from Quadro Caminos, and is well graded. The views are excellent from both sides of the road; firstly over the plains around Xela, and higher up of the volcanoes. Nearer the top pine forest starts to predominate up the highest point (km170 AKA Alaska) where it can be very chilly and windy. Descending, there are beautiful views of the patchwork of milpa fields around Nahaula.

The highland town of **Nahuala** is an interesting place to stop, not many tourists come by, and those that do are usually pleasantly ignored. It's one of the few places where the men have retained their costumes, wearing simple brown woollen 'kilts', and embroidered shirts. The Sunday market is lively, bringing in people from a wide area. Onwards to the lake, head out of town and rejoin the Pan-American Highway.

It descends for a few km, before climbing to the turning right near the km148 marker. There's a steepish 5km climb, up to the ridge around the lake with incredible views off to the left at the Mirador del Suenos. Then it's a long steep descent, through the forest followed by a short 2km climb up to Sta Maria. Onwards there are stunning views all the way down the 20 switchbacks to the lake, there's another short climb up into San Pablo la Laguna.

Lago Atitlan

To describe it at length with words would do an injustice, it is a natural wonder of the world. Simply, it's a big beautiful lake, surrounded by mountains and volcanoes.

The boats that criss-cross the lake are quick, cheap and quite regular, although paying an extra standard fare for bikes is normal. Different rates apply for locals and tourists.

There are many walks and trails around the lakeshore, or up the coffee lined volcanoes and mountainsides.

NB Ask locally for current safety advice as robbery and theft are regularly reported in areas around the lake

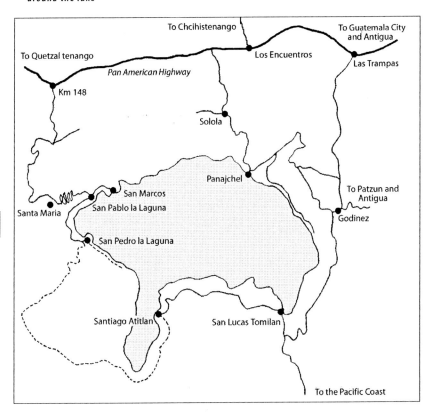

Panajchel – Aka Pana, is the most developed lakeside town for tourists, with banks, internet facilities and a wide range of accommodation to suit most budgets. There are tourist markets and shops, with the usual regional handicrafts and textiles. The older part of town, is further away from the lake and has the usual food and produce markets with some cheap comedors at the back. A side trip to Santa Catarina and San Antonio Palopo, will give excellent lake views from a different perspective. The paved road up to Solola is narrow and can be busy, it would be tough climb, although the views are excellent almost all the way. There are regular buses.

Solola – This traditional town is one the few places where the men still wear their traditional dress, being colourful trousers and embroidered shirts. It's well worth making the effort for

68

one of the markets on Tuesday or Friday.

There are a couple of places to stay, although there's much more choice in Panajchel.

San Pedro la Laguna – A short hop by launch from Panajchel, or via the descent along the road from km 148 on the Pan American, passing through San Pablo.

The town itself is quite traditional, and has a reasonable market in the centre, along with a couple of banks and shops for supplies. It caters well for budget travellers', and is one of the cheapest place for Spanish lessons. It's a good place to meet people in the variety of bars and restaurants. The dirt track which heads east out of town along the lakeshore is worth exploring, in town the steep cobbled streets are not very bike friendly, although there are a maze of footpaths. The jetty for boats to Panajchel and villages on the north side of the lake, the other is a couple of km away on the other side of town, for boats to Santiago Atitlan.

San Marcos – Can be reached by launch from Panajchel, or follow the road down from 'km148' on the Pan American highway via San Pablo (check your brakes first!). The views are stunning on this descent. It's one of the nicest places in Guatemala to completely relax, with it's holistic centres, rustic accommodations and cafes. There are several shaded footpaths from the village centre leading through the coffee plants to the lakeside. Many come and find it hard to leave!

San Pablo de la Laguna – For most it's a place to pass through on the way to San Marcos or San Pedro, or to wait for pick-ups to Santa Maria, however there is nice plaza in front of the church with good views over the lake.

San Lucas Tomilan – This traditional settlement is pleasant to pass through without having much to detain the average traveller. There are a few comedors if wanting a meal break and attractive lake views from the shore.

Santiago Atitlan – This is another interesting village that looks after an effigy of Maximon, and all the rituals associated with it. There are several shops and stalls selling local handicrafts, to cater for the many day-trippers. If wanting to spend the night, there are a couple of places to stay.

Lago Atitlan–Antigua

There are a 3 possibilities outlined to get to Antigua, each is unique with different scenery.

1) Via the Pacific Highway and Vol. Acatenango about 130km

This route has stunning views from the ridges around Vol. Acatenengo. The route was researched the other way round, and will probably need a bit of pick-up or bus help to do in a day.

From the west side of the lake, take the boat or cycle around Vol. San Pedro (check locally as to whether the route is currently safe) to Santiago Atitlan. This is an interesting, but touristy town to stop a while. Then there's a pretty 15km ride on a paved surface, through the coffee plantations to San Lucas Toliman. The next 35km to Cocales junction are almost entirely downhill, and pass through everchanging scenery to the hot Pacific plains.

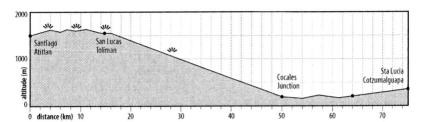

The Pacific highway is busy with heavy traffic, although there is space at the side of the road to cycle, if possible try to get a bus for the 23km to **Sta Lucia Cotzumalguapa**. There are some interesting ancient Pipil ruins nearby and accommodation if needing to stop over.

Climbing the back of Vol. Acatenango is a long 2000m climb, if not wanting such a daunting prospect, there is regular transport up to Yepocapa, which is more than half-way and cooler for cycling. Onwards are one or two early morning buses to Antigua.

The dirt road is well graded and winds around the side of the volcano, with ever changing lush vegetation giving some shade. There are some small settlements, with basic shops, and surrounded by coffee plantations. The soils are very fertile, and further up the land has been cleared for agriculture, giving excellent views (cloud permitting). Eventually the road reaches La Soledad (shops), where the footpath for climbing the volcano starts.

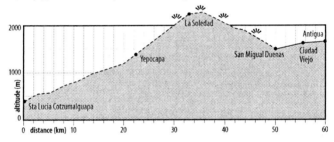

Onward routes are covered by the ITMB inset map of Guatemala City and surrounds.
After another couple of km, the road starts to descend to a dusty village. Onwards there is a choice of routes into Antigua:
The descent to San Miguel Duenas, then a 100m climb up to Cuidad Viejo on a paved road, and onto Antigua;
Or via Parramos, involving another climb after the San Miguel junction, followed by a long dusty descent to Parramos, then down the highway into Antigua.

2) Via Patizicia, Patzun and San Andreas Ixtapa, about 85km
NB The road from Godinez to Patzun used to carry a warning for robbery in guidebooks. It does seem to be safe these days. Best check locally in Godinez for the current situation.
The highlights of this journey are the incredible views from Xepatan, up and down the line of volcanos, there are also some pretty woodland sections.

This is one journey to start early, there is a lot to enjoy and a couple of significant climbs. The 600m climb out of Panajchel to Godinez, is a well graded and steady climb. There are good views over the lake almost the entire way, as the road clings to the mountain side in places.
Godinez is a functional place for food and refreshment. The route continues through town and is well signed to Patzun as it begins a long descent into a deep valley.

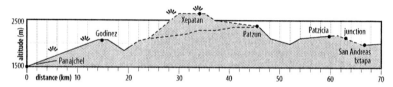

After crossing the river, it's possible to cycle directly to Patzun by continuing on the paved road, however this misses the spectacular views from the mountain ridge near Xepatan.
The turning to this village is off to the right, after a short climb. This road then drops back down to cross the river a second time. The climb up to Xepatan is long and steep in places on dirt or badly paved roads, it will necessary to ask directions occasionally and there are a couple of villages on the way with shops for supplies and refreshment. The views are excellent on the climb and the mountainsides are covered in patchwork agriculture, with a few copses of woodland. At the top there is a long grassy ridge with excellent views (clouds permitting) up and down the chain of volcanos. Xepatan has a couple of shops, but no comedors. There's a dusty descent off the ridge, then a short ride across the agricultural plains to **Patzun**. The settlement is spread along the road to the left, and has little of interest unless hungry.
Onwards the road drops into a beautiful pine forested valley, with a river running alongside, a great place for a picnic is the grassy area by the bridge. Climbing out of this valley, the road straightens out passing through rich agricultural land. **Patzicia**, the next town is functional, but unexciting, there's a short climb up to Pan American highway, and then a few km along it to the Zaragoza junction. From this point use the route description to San Andreas Ixtapa and Antigua at the end of route 3).

3) Via the Ixmiche ruins near Tecpan, Comalapa and San Andreas Ixtapa 120km

This route involves the same beautiful 600m climb from Panajchel up to Godinez as in route 2). Then another 18km undulating climb toward the Pan-American highway at Las Trampas. It's a 20km stretch on the Pan American, which although through pretty, forested ridges, may be better bussed if the traffic is bad.

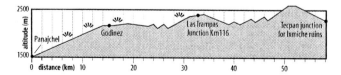

An easier way from Panajchel or San Pedro, is to take a bus to Guatemala City, and ask to be dropped at Tecpan.
Tecpan is just off the Pan American highway and the Ixmiche ruins are 5km south of the town, whilst not as impressive as other ruins in the region, they're important to the local Kakquichel people.

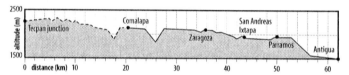

To Comalapa, return to the Pan-American highway. A couple of hundred metres to the south of the Tecpan junction, there's a dirt track off to the left, which is not well marked, ask if unsure. This follows a very beautiful valley, before climbing into more open countryside. There are numerous, small peaceful settlements, and the pine forest is mixed with small-scale farming. There are several climbs, some steep, although none very long. The crossing points of the rivers, marked on the ITMB map, have some meadow ideal for discreet camping.

Comalapa is a pleasant town and artistic centre, with many studios having art on display. There are also a few murals, one stretches for a couple of hundred metres. Basic accommodation is available if needed. The road onwards is now paved all the way, and negotiates a deep pine forested valley, before climbing more gently over the rich agricultural plains to **Zaragoza** near the Pan-American Highway.

Onwards is covered by the larger scale ITMB inset map of Antigua and surrounds
The track to San Andreas Ixtapa (unmarked on the ITMB map), is just over the Pan American from the Zaragoza turning, it starts off paved, before quickly becoming an earth track, that then disappears around farmland and woodland for 5km, once on the track it's difficult to get lost, and there are usually local farmers around to ask directions. It climbs briefly, then descends to eventually cross a stream at the back of San Andreas, before climbing steeply into the settlement.

San Andreas Ixtapa – is one of a few towns that hosts an effigy of San Simon. It isn't entirely approved of by the Church, but the people keep coming! There is a small charge to enter the building, 3 blocks north of the plaza. Cigars, candles, alcohol, and other small niknaks are the usual offerings, for the good favour of this renegade saint.

This was one of the few towns obliterated by the 1976 earthquake and the concrete buildings that replaced the traditional adobe and pan tile shacks are not pretty.

The short cut to Parramos, goes from 100m above the petrol station at the bottom of town, and is partially paved, it crosses over a small bridge, before passing through market garden agricultural fields. From Parramos the road is level for a couple of km, before dropping through a valley to Pastores. It's then a gentle descent through Jocotenango and into Antigua.

Antigua
This beautiful city was once the colonial capital of Central America, and is now a major tourist destination. Nestled in between 3 volcanoes, with wonderful architecture, cobbled streets, courtyard gardens and beautiful churches. There is a wide choice of accommodation, a vibrant bar and cafe culture, and some excellent bookshops. If wanting to cycle with a group, mountain bike tours are offered locally by the Old town outfitters (1 block south of the plaza).

It's easily the most popular destination for learning Spanish in the region, there are dozens of schools, with a variety of programmes, from staying with families to private tuition and classes.
NB See the inset on the ITMB map for a street plan of Antigua, some hotel locations are also given

The nearby suburb town of Jocotenango, is a short ride up toward Chimaltenango, and is (foreign) tourist free if needing to escape the hoards in Antigua.

The cross above Antigua (opposite side to Vol. Agua) can be visited easily by bike or on foot, for superb views of the whole city and the surroundings.

The volcanoes around Antigua are all climbable, although **Vol.Fuego** will require the services of a guide. Many tourists who try to climb **Vol.Agua** on their own get mugged (or worse), it is inadvisable to go unless with an organised group. This situation may change in the next few years if a similar scheme to that on Pacaya is set up.

Vol. Acatenango has much less criminal activity and is an incredible trip; it's worth camping overnight for the sunset and dawn views. (☞ see p.75)

Vol. Pacaya is now a much safer trip to make independently, as the locals now make a small income from every tourist. The nicest route is via Sta Maria de Jesus, and Palin, before climbing up to San Vicente and the start of the footpaths at San Francisco. For company it might be worth latching on to an organised group for the walk.

There are several companies that offer tours, some with overnight camping, especially worth it if the volcano is very active.

NB If wanting to travel independently, weekends are safer as there are plenty of Guatemalan climbers as well, try to link up with another group if possible. Shoes with a good grip are essential, as the steep paths are covered with loose volcanic dust.

Chimaltenango on the Pan American highway is a place that most tourists will only ever know as the place to get bus connections to, from Antigua. It's a good place for bike shops, and has a large Friday market that is completely tourist-free, but there is little else of interest to make it worth staying overnight.

There is a new road from El Tejar to Antigua not marked on the ITMB map

☞ see p.69-72 for 3 routes to **Lago Atitlan**, described in reverse.

SIDE TRIPS

1) To Monterrico via Santa Maria Jesus

This is a nice getaway from Antigua, to the black sands of the Pacific coast, relaxing on the beach, paddles through the mangroves, and beautiful sunsets.

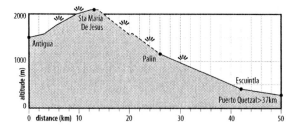

The most interesting way is via **Santa Maria de Jesus** on the slopes of Vol. Agua (The market on Sunday makes visiting this village a nice morning round trip from Antigua) and then down the dirt road to Palin, this is an exciting descent, with wonderful views over to Vol. Pacaya and forested scenery.

Palin market is worth a quick look, mainly for the enormous ceiba tree covering it. From there, continue down the main road to Escuintla, the temperature will climb steadily. The next section has been turned into a 4-lane road, across the hot, monotonous Pacific plains. There

are few chances of refreshment, so it's worth taking one of the regular buses for the 45km to Ixtapa. If taking a bus to Puerto Quetzal, get off at the intersection for Itztapa, and head east down the coast, surprisingly there is a bike track! Cycle through the centre of Itztapa, and cross the canal on the other side by ferry to the coastal road for Monterrico (There may be a bridge in the next few years). This quiet road is a relaxing ride, with the sea never far away and sometimes a pleasant seabreeze, there are a few villages along the way for refreshments.

Monterrico is a wonderfully simple resort, although it is growing quickly. There are several reasonably priced beachfront hotels and backpackers lodgings to choose from, along with bars and restaurants. Nearby is a hatchery for turtles and reptiles to visit, and excursions by boat or canoe through the mangroves.

Return the same way or....
...take the ferry through the mangroves to La Avellena and cycle up to the Pacific highway at Taxisco. Then back to Escuintla or....

... via Chiquimulilla, Culiapa, and then the 40km on the main highway before cutting through to Vol. Pacaya and Palin via Sta Elena Barillas.
See the larger scale ITMB inset of Antigua and surrounds.

It may be better to take a bus from Chiquimulilla to Culiapa, and onto the turn off (for Sta Elena Barillas), it's an easier way of gaining height and these can be busy roads. Mention to the bus driver to make sure he knows where to stop. The ride to Palin is on a mix of dirt and paved roads, passing through coffee plantations, with good views over Lago de Amatitlan.
NB The area around Lago Amitlan has a bad reputation for robbery and this would not be a good road to be stuck on at night, allow at least 4 hours for cycling through to Palin.
At San Francisco, halfway along, there are footpaths for the climb up to the still active **Vol. Pacaya.** This was once a dangerous volcano to climb, but now the villagers levy a small tourist tax and make some money legitimately from tourism.

It's then all downhill to Palin, from where it's a stiff climb back up to Sta Maria de Jesus, or a pick-up ride from near the market, followed by a relaxing descent to Antigua.

2) To the Mixco Viejo ruins, 110km round trip
This is an interesting ride through some less visited parts of the country, with a wonderful variety of scenery.

Purely cycled it's a very tough, long day in the saddle, to save 30km and avoid the busy roads, take an early bus to San Martin Jilotepeque, best on a Sunday for the market. Stock up

with water and food as the next section has no shops, and head north, up and out of town. After a couple km there's a marked turning to Mixco Viejo on the right. From this point to the ruins it's almost entirely level or downhill, and the dirt roads are in good condition. At the first obvious fork (unsigned) bear left and continue through the ranch and scrubland. The next junction is a crossroads in a small settlement. There is a public water tap if needed (it's the last chance for free water for some time), as it's very hot in this dry valley. Turn right, there are a few turn-offs on this road, but keep descending until joining the paved road. Turn left, crossing the river and climb for a couple of km to the ruins.

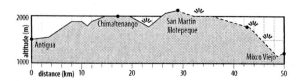

Mixco Viejo has been tastefully restored, and the dry land site is very interesting. During the week the ruins will be very quiet, at the weekend there are more visitors from the city, which can be useful if wanting a better chance of a lift up the long climb toward San Pedro Sacatepequez.
NB There are only very limited refreshments available on site and no shops nearby.

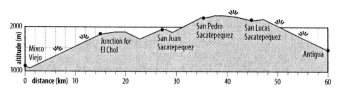

The 1200m climb out of this valley up to San Pedro Sacatepequez is long and hard because of the heat. For the first few km there are very few opportunities for refreshment and little shade, although increasingly good views behind. At the top of the first part of the climb, there are junctions to El Chol and San Raymundo. Onwards there's thicker pine forest, which gives some shade. The road becomes busier at times, and starts to descend into a narrow valley, then there's a steady climb up the other side to San Juan Sacatepequez. This town has a pleasant square, and is a nice place for a break, as there's another 5km of climbing up to **San Pedro Sacatepequez.**

This town has a lot of character, with a large church and markets, it's easy to lose a sense of direction, as the streets wind around the mountain slopes. There is accommodation if needed. *The following routes are included on the large scale inset of Antigua and the Capital on the ITMB map.*
From San Pedro Sacatepequez, it's downhill which ever you go:
To the Capital – It's another 20km, as the winding road descends out of the forest, and into the suburbs of the city.
To Antigua – It's a pretty ride, through rich agricultural lands to San Lucas Sacatepequez, these roads are now paved, and then the long fast descent down the 4-lane highway into Antigua. Or another route to Antigua is via Zenacoj, and through more pine forest. There's a steep valley to negotiate after Zenacoj, before a short stretch on the Pan American highway to Sumpango. From there turn right, the last section is a descent through thick dust on the dirt roads to Jocotenango on the outskirts of Antigua.

3) Vol. Acatenango, 28km, +4-5 hours hard climbing to the summit
This route is the easiest way to cycle to Soledad, where the footpath to the summit of Vol. Acatenango starts.
Cycle or bus to Parramos, on the main highway, and turn left (opposite the road to Chimaltenango). This road quickly becomes dust, and starts to climb with a reasonable gradients, through the agricultural landscape. It's 16km to Soledad, with a 2km descent after 10km. After passing the turn off left to San Miguel Duenas, there is a steepish climb up to a

75

ridge, the views up and down the chain of volcanos are outstanding. The road then gently descends into Soledad.

   The path to the summit starts a couple of hundred metres south of the village. Allow for 5 hours hard climbing to the top, shoes with a good grip are essential. The marking of paths is being improved all the time. Camping at the top is fine with a good sleeping bag and tent, dawn is unforgettable, especially if Vol. Fuego is active a few km away. If on your own, it's best climbed at the weekend when there are plenty of tourists and locals around.
NB Take several litres of water, there is none on the climb.
There are a couple of shops in Soledad; the one below the road is the best for bike storage.
There are buses from Antigua to Soledad (marked either to Yepocapa or Acatenango), just cycling back is nice way to finish the trip.
☞ see p.70 for a part of a X-section of Antigua to Soledad via San Miguel Duenas

4) San Andreas Ixtapa loop, 53 km round trip
Cycle or bus to Parramos, on the main highway, and turn left in the village, at the end of the plaza (opposite the road toward Chimaltenango). This road quickly becomes dust, and starts to climb with reasonable gradients, although there are a couple of steeper sections.
   The views are pretty, being mainly highland agriculture, with some woodand in between, At the high point after 10km from Parramos, there's a junction, turn right and climb steeply for another 1.5km. The views on this ridge are superb, there's a good place to relax just off the road to the right. Decending, at the next village, bear left (although either route will drop down to Ixtapa) descending through woodland, pasture and milpa, take the next right, passing through the rustic hamlet of Chicasanga, and down to **San Andreas Ixtapa**.
   This town is unremarkable, except for being a base for the cult of San Simon (Maximom). His effigy is housed 3 blocks north of the plaza, ask if unsure. He can be visited for a fee, and offerings of cigars, candles, alcohol or other trinkets are expected in return for good fortune!
   Continuing on, drop through town, and take a right turn 100m above the petrol station, at the base of town, this road goes directly back to Parramos, through agricultural plantations, then it's the same way back.
All roads are shown on the large scale ITMB map inset of Antigua and surrounds

Antigua to Guatemala City to Antigua – The 4 lane highway from the Capital to San Lucas is the busiest road in the country, and is now 4 lanes wide nearly all the way to Chimaltenango. There are big climbs in both directions, and the pollution can be pretty bad, particularly on the climb out of the capital.

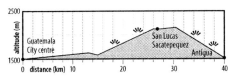

If taking a bus from Guatemala City, get off at San Lucas Sacatepequez, after a short climb, the 4-lane road is a fast downhill all the way into Antigua, with excellent views. Spare the Latin machismo, and don't overtake too many cars!

Guatemala City aka Guate
The city plan on the ITMB map is good enough for getting about
This is a noisy, dirty and chaotic city, for most people it's enough just to pass through,

changing buses, and spending as little time as possible. On a bike, it saves endless tramping, although the pollution is pretty bad. It can be a dangerous place, and there have been an increasing number of hi-jackings and robberies involving guns, if possible explore having left valuables in a safe place.

On the bright side there are some incredible markets, with the widest selection of merchandise in Central America. Any expensive bike parts should be available from one of the specialist bike shops, Zones 10 and 15 are the wealthier districts and the best places to look. There is every type of accommodation available in Zone1, if needed.

Nearly all the better quality buses go from the streets near the old train station in Zone 1, the terminal for buses to Antigua is a few blocks north. The cheaper bus terminal is by the big markets in Zone 4.

Guatemala city–Chiquimula–Honduras

This main road to the Caribbean, is one that is easy to recommend taking a bus for, it's very busy and has little space. Cycling from Zacapa or Chiquimula are reasonable options, it's a nice ride of nearly 70km to Copan ruinas from the later.

Chiquimula to Copan Ruinas – The first part on the main road is 10km gently uphill to the junction at Vado Honda, the road then climbs through a dry landscape, with no shade but good views from the pass. Descending the other side, San Juan Ermita has a couple of comedors and is a nice place for a break.

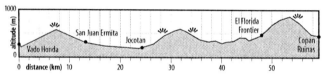

The road continues undulating gently down the river valley toward Jocotan. This larger settlement is a short detour off the main road. Shortly after is a nice climb over a shady forested ridge with good views on both sides. To the border the road undulates alongside the river through farmland and small settlements, it is particularly pretty at sunset with the sun setting into the mountains behind.

The frontier is just uphill of the small village of El Florido, and straight forward as plenty of people will direct you if looking lost. There are exit and entrance 'taxes' although little more than a couple of dollars. Plenty of money changers are on hand offering poor exchange rates, this might be useful if crossing on the weekend, although it's normally easy to find someone to change dollars at a better rate in Copan Ruinas.

The introduction to Honduras is a stiff climb, with no shade, although there are some good views from the top, before enjoying the downhill to Copan Ruinas town.

☞ see p.94 for Copan Ruinas

Chiquimula to Esquipulas and onto Nueva Octepeque (Honduras), 75km – This main road can be busy, preferably it's better to bus straight to Esquipulas, and enjoy the riding with less traffic from there. If deciding to ride, the dryland scenery is attractive, although it can be a hot climb, and there is little shade.

Esquipulas is worth a couple of hours, it's a place of pilgrimage and has many thousands of visitors with a large numbers of comedors to keep them fed. The church is the main focus of attention for the faithful, and there are candle and trinkets sellers lining the roads.

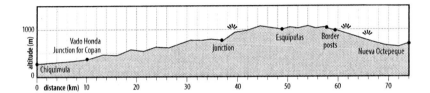

From Esquipulas the climbing has almost been done, just a gentle undulating climb up to the Guatemalan frontier. Formalities are simple, before a short km downhill to the Honduran border, at Agua Caliente. This can be a little more chaotic as it has been the main route for illegal migration in the past, the entrance fee is usually no more than a couple of dollars. Unless it's the weekend, it's not worth dealing with the money changers. Enjoy the peaceful downhill through the pine forest, there some good views into the deep side valleys. One of the first impressions is the number of attractive pan tiled homes. Once over the bridge at the bottom, there's a short climb over a small ridge into Neuva Ocotepeque. Go to Pg 97

Peten

The home of beautiful ruins, verdant jungle and ranchland plains. It's hot and mostly flat with bands of steep sided small hills making the cycling more interesting. The distances between places can be longer, so the occasional bus/pickup ride over more monotonous sections makes sense.

Due to higher transport costs, some things are a little more expensive than elsewhere in Guatemala. There is a slightly rougher frontier attitude (cowboys!!) in some places.

Belizean Border (Melchor Mencos) to Remate to Melchor Mencos, 65km – There is some forest on this route, but the area has mostly been cleared for cattle ranches. There are a few settlements straggling the road, which is now close to being paved, the whole way (beware a few large potholes). Half way along are the isolated Yaxcha ruins.

Yaxcha (Yaxha or Yaxja) ruins 20km detour
Take plenty of water; the only chance for more is to re-fill with local water by the security barrier at the lakeside. The dirt road is in reasonable condition, with a couple of small hills to negotiate. Cross the spit between the lakes, and climb again for 3km. The ruins are well marked and there are some low-key entrance buildings. The ruins are gradually being restored, and walking through the thinned wooded glades is a very pleasing, peaceful experience. It's unusual to see more than a handful of people, and the views from the tops of two of the pyramids are superb. Coming back, the climb up from the lake is hard in the heat. There is an Ecolodge on the southside of lake, and camping is possible.

The road to Remate continues, there are a couple of small hills and more undulation, the first signs of arrival are glimpses of a lake to the north of the road, after a few more km, the junction with the Flores-Tikal road is reached. Turn right for places to stay (1-2km), and excellent views of Lake Peten Itza.

Remate
This village is very laid-back and the sunsets are particularly beautiful. There are rapidly

increasing number of cabanas, hotels, and comedors, most with good views over the lake. The small **Cerro Cahui National Park**, 2km down the dirt road to San Jose is worth a visit. There are a few different paths through the forest, and good views from the lookouts.

Remate to Tikal, 33km – Leaving early from Remate, allow 2.5-3 hrs in order to get to the ruins. There is a stiff climb up from the lake to another settlement, then the road undulates through ranchland and a few smaller communities to the national park entrance at the halfway point. There is a comedor, on the right, the last chance for cheap food.

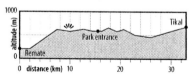

Onwards, into the park are two short and one longish climbs to the ruins. There is regular traffic, but plenty of gaps to enjoy the sights and noises of the forest.

A pleasant compromise would be to use a minibus to get to Tikal for the sunrise and cycle back later at leisure.

Tikal
The ruins and area around them are unmissable (if possible). The temples and other structures are beautifully made, and the views from the tops of the pyramids are unforgettable. It's easy to spend a whole day amongst the ruins, and many try to spend a night as well. This is officially not allowed and getting harder, as the security has been improved to prevent robberies. The wildlife is superb and it's not unusual to see troops of monkeys, toucans and other animals.

Staying near the ruins is possible, either reasonably priced camping or in one of the hotels. Food is predictably expensive, and there are no shops, so bring what you need if on a budget. *NB Unfortunately, no cycling is allowed around the site, it's a shame as it would be an excellent way for getting to the outlying ruins.*

Onwards the 25km dirt road to the ruins at Uaxactun, is usually in reasonable condition, except after heavy rain and mostly under shade. It hasn't been researched, but has been a tempting possibility, along with the track from there down to the bat caves and ruins at El Zotz. With time it's possible to continue and make a circular route back to San Jose on Lago Peten Itza. Take enough supplies to be self sufficient and ask locally for advice on track conditions, as getting stuck on a remote section won't be much fun.

Remate to Flores/San Elena, (via San Jose) 30km – There are two options:
The easiest – is along the paved road passing the airport, the route is uninteresting, but quick.
The more interesting – is a beautiful journey along the north side of the lake to San Jose.
There are 2 or three hills on this dirt road, rough in places, but very rideable. There is very little traffic, although increasing numbers of holiday homes and hotels are being built. A couple of villages are passed through, with surrounding milpa and the rest is forested.

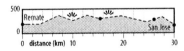

From San Jose it's possible to get launches across the lake to Flores. These are cheap, although the bike will be extra. The regular launches stop running at dusk, though it's possible to charter one at a price.

Flores
A pretty colonial town built on an island at the edge of a beautiful lake. It's connected to Santa Elena by a short causeway. The old pan tiles have been gradually replaced by painted tin, but the old buildings and narrow streets are still authentic. It's worth a cycle round, there are a mix of hotels, shops and internet facilities, although for visiting Tikal by bike, Remate is a better place to stay. There are launches across the lake to San Jose from the west side of the island.

San Elena/San Benito
The modern neighbour towns to Flores, with all the conveniences like banks, bike shops etc. There are some large covered markets at the back of the bus station, which are worth a look if having some time to kill.

   It's also where all the long distance buses go from, with several different lines direct to Guatemala City and Antigua. Also there are buses to the Mexican border at Co-op Bethel, the Belizean border at Melchor Mencos and Sayaxche on the route to Coban.

Flores–Belize
Follow the 30km highway to Remate, turn right at the junction there and then
☞ see p.78 for a decription of the route in reverse.

Flores–Poptun
Flores/San Benito to Poptun, 115km – The road is now paved all the way, and the journey to Rio Dulce is best broken at about half way at the Finca Ixobel, Poptun.
   It's about 10km past the airport, to the junction for the new highway south. The road gently

climbs over several small hills, through mainly ranchland, there isn't much shade, but occasional roadside settlements have refreshments for cooling off. It gets prettier and more interesting through the steep sided, forested hills south of Sabaneta, with some shade in the early morning or late afternoon. There are a lot of ups and downs, but the views and scenery are fantastic, nearer **Poptun** the road starts to flatten out. This town is growing rapidly, there isn't a great deal for the average tourist, although there are banks and basic accommodations near the market if needed.

Finca Ixobel is south of the town, involving a trek over (or around) the airfield, and a couple more km on the main road, the turning right is well marked. It's then another km on a track to the farm. There is a variety of accommodation from camping to individual rooms, at reasonable prices. The food is excellent, and there are many excursions from caving to horse riding (padded cycle shorts work well with the hard western saddles).

Poptun to Rio Dulce, 100km – There are several climbs, the biggest in the first 15km to San Luis, with many of the typically steep sided, tree topped hills of the region. The views in the early morning are excellent.

Onwards, is uncycled, but the scenery is very similar to the rest of the journey from Flores, the highway gradually flattens out for the last hot 30km, there are regular road side settlements with shops for food and water.

☞ see p.91 for **Rio Dulce**.

Poptun–Coban

Poptun to Fray Bartolome de las Casas (about 100km) and onto Coban – This is the prettiest route to Coban from Peten There's a long climb up into the mountains nearer Coban, however this route is stunning and would be the highlight of the trip.

The ITMB map is ok for navigating on this route, although it is difficult to get lost, as there is only one main dirt road, and few junctions

From Poptun, its 16km south on the highway, climbing over a ridge of hills to San Luis, then turn right through this settlement for dirt roads the rest of the way. At first are many small ranchitos and further on, a lot of land has been cleared for large fields of maize, although there are some amazing rocky outcrops covered in forest and many small villages.

The road is mostly good compressed gravel, and descends through foothills from San Luis. The scenery around the halfway point of the journey is particularly beautiful, as the road climbs and falls around lush steep sided hills. For the 20km nearer Fray Bartoleme, it's flatter and easy to make quick progress, although watch for the dust of occasional passing vehicles.

There is one bus a day servicing this route, leaving from near the market in Poptun sometime between 8 and 9.30 in the morning.

☞ see p.84 for **Fray Bartoleme de las Casas**

Flores–Coban via Sayaxche

Flores to Sayaxche, 55km – This road is gradually being paved, which is just as well as the dust from passing cars can be choking. It isn't the prettiest route either, though easy being mostly flat. There is some heavy traffic, connected with oil exploration just off the road, and a few small settlements. The scenery is mainly dry scrubland, with remnants of forest, and many large cattle ranches. Nearer Sayaxche is the turning right to Co-op Bethel and the Mexican border, and after are a few small hills for the last few km.

There is a river crossing into **Sayaxche**, with several small launches which don't look bike friendly, or the slow car and truck barge, which is a feat of engineering. One day, no doubt, there will be a bridge, which will change the character of this town completely. At present, it's a

pleasant river port, there are some cheap and basic rooms and a hotel, a stones throw from the river. It's possible to arrange launch trips up and down the river, but obviously much cheaper in a group.

SIDE TRIP
El Ceibal ruins, 40km round trip
This is a nice side trip to some quiet, tourist free ruins. Take the road south for 9km, and turn left. There is an 8km rough dirt road through lush vegetation to the ruins, with some small climbs. The ruins are well kept, though not spectacular, the surrounding forest though is beautiful and is relatively undisturbed. There's a warden, and some ongoing restoration. An alternative would be a launch ride to the hill below the ruins, though it could be expensive, unless with a group.
Camping nearby is possible, although the mosquitoes are notoriously thirsty.

Sayaxche to Cruce El Pato, 71km – This road will soon be paved all the way, at present there are just a few very dusty sections. Scenery-wise this route is flat and dull; ranches, scrub, and a few settlements straggle along the road, which is dead straight for almost 40km. Returning refugees from Mexico from the civil war were offered parcels of land along side it as part of resettlement packages.
NB There has been a recent discovery of extensive ruins at Cancuen, close to El Cruce del Pato, some of the finds seem to contradict traditional views of ancient Mayan society, including signs of a matriachy. This site is not yet open to the public.
Cruce el Pato is at the junction of the road toward Rubelsanto and Laguna Lachua, and very much a place to just pass through. Starting early and taking a pick-up or microbus makes sense, to give time to get to Fray Bartoleme, Laguna Lachua, or explore the nearby Chinaja national park

Chinaja National Park
The ITMB map doesn't show all the routes in these mountains
This park is completely off the tourist trail, and quite special. The dirt road up to the park starts a 5 km west of Cruce del Pato. After a few minutes climbing through the forest, the track emerges through a cutting and descends into a clearing, with a village. The people are friendly, and a shopkeeper may agree to look after your panniers whilst you're exploring the mountains.

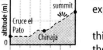

There is one road climbing out from the other end of the village, this twists and turns through the forest, climbing all the time. Nearer the top, is a junction, the one to the left goes to a dead end on the ridge. The other goes to a telecoms tower, and potentially has better views. The only way down is the same way, the tracks are rough, and good off-roading.

Cruce el Pato to Coban – There are two longer, interesting routes, via Lanquin or the laguna Lachua. A quicker more direct route, is via Chisec, this is now paved all the way, although this still involves crossing several valleys in the climb up to Coban.

1) To Coban via the Laguna Lachua
This route involves a uninteresting flat section toward Rubelsanto, followed by prettier road through the characteristic steep sided hills of this region, nearer Laguna Lachua is thick forest. The route back to towards Coban is tough, but beautiful, through the small forested hills.

Cruce el Pato to Laguna Lachua National Park, 80km – Turning left along the northern edge of the Chinaja range, the road bends north west and undulates gently through the jungle scrub and milpas, for 18km. At the next junction, there is a small settlement, head left; there are some pretty sections on this ride, but lots of monotonous bits as well. Take the next right to Rubelsanto; this area has some oil exploration, a pipeline sits beside the road, and there are occasional tankers.

In Rubelsanto, turn left and check directions, as the roads can be misleading. Onwards the ride becomes much more interesting, the scenery more forested with the familiar hillocks of this area. There are only a one or two small settlements, and the forest becomes denser as the road undulates over small streams nearer the national park entrance.

NB With limited time getting a pick-up (if possible!) to Rubelsanto is a reasonable idea.

Laguna Lachua national park

At the entrance to the park is a cabin with wardens who can help with queries about the walk to the lake, the area around it, and local accommodations. Camping is possible nearby..

The lake is in a beautiful forested setting, and there is a good diversity of bird and animal life.

Playa Grande is the river port, near the Laguna Lachua and there is a large army base on the west side of the river. Areas further west are frontier territory, not necessarily dangerous, just be on your guard as the attitude is rougher. There is an interesting unresearched route onwards to Barillas, ask locally for up-to-date advice and information.

Laguna Lachua to Coban, at least 120km – *This route is not shown on the ITMB map*
It would be easy to underestimate the time to cycle this route, as this journey would be a very long hard day if attempted in one go, getting a lift from the Chisec road to Coban, or camping out are the alternatives.

This is a beautiful journey, but with an incredible number of climbs up and down the steep sided hills of the area, and the varying scenery is a bit special. The first part undulates gently through the forest, the road then emerges into a mixed agricultural landscape, with the road winding around the forested hillocks that make this area distinct. Climbing around the edge of them can be very difficult after rain, even the 4x4s struggle! There are very few shops for supplies after passing Saholom, so stock up where possible.

Eventually the road follows a river valley down to the Chisec road at Cuibilhuitz. Onwards it's about 40km to Coban, the paved road predominately climbs, passing through several valleys in a pretty forested landscape. Microbuses (with roofracks) and other transport ply the route to Coban until dusk, if needed.

2) To Coban via Lanquin and Semuc Champey

This route involves a flat paved road to Fray Bartolome, followed by a long climb on dirt roads through the beautiful mountain scenery to Pajal junction, for Lanquin and the cascades at Semuc Champey. Onwards to Coban are excellent views over the valleys below, the road is being widened and will no doubt be paved in the near future.

Cruce El Pato to Fray Bartolome de las Casas, 99km – This road has now been paved and is the preferred route to Coban. It's a straight forward 19km to the junction for Chisec, and another 25 km to Fray Bartolome de las Casas. These hot roads undulate gentle, there are views of the Chinaja mountains, although the roadside scenery is uninteresting, being mainly scrub vegetation and ranchland, stock up on supplies where possible as there are long gaps between settlements.

There are regular microbuses (with roofracks) from the junction with the Chisec road onwards.

Fray Bartolome de las Casas aka Fray is not a tourist destination, however it is a useful staging post for onward travel. The settlement straggles a wide road for a couple of km, and there a couple of quite reasonable places to stay, although the hospedaje across from the market takes 'basic' to a new level!

The central highlands

Fray Bartolome de las Casas to Lanquin, about 60km– It's a long 1000+m climb up to Pajal, the junction for Lanquin. However the varied scenery is very beautiful and the views through the tight valleys are incredible. The dirt road is rough in places, and cut into a mountainside with abundant lush vegetation There are a few small agricultural settlements in the hills, with basic shops. On the flatter sections, there are small ranches, on the steep slopes, milpa, coffee and cardamom. In reality, the mountains are often covered in mist or cloud, so if wishing to enjoy this climb from a bus, there is one a day, leaving early from Fray Bartolome.

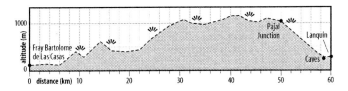

Lanquin and Semuc Champey

Definately worth a visit, even if the thought of climbing back from the bottom of the valley is too much. Lanquin town is becoming a backpack haven, and is a nice place to relax. There is a variety of basic accommodation, and several local excursions.

The entrance to the caves is on the road to Coban, 2km outside town. For tight budgets, peace and quiet, and good swimming, there's a palapa near the cave entrance by the river, it's free for hanging hammocks. The caves are well lit and it's possible to walk for several minutes, through the different caverns, often with sounds of rushing water below. The river which formed the caves, has made itself a lower path through the limestone and the water when it emerges from the rock is very cold, but unpolluted, and excellent for a refreshing swim.

Semuc Champey, is a short 10km away, however in between is a steep 400m climb. There are regular pick-ups, other transport, for some time out of the saddle. These rapids are an awesome sight, with the whole river disappearing underground, above are some beautiful pools for swimming. The surrounding forested countryside is also a treat. There are a couple of palapas for camping and hammocks, which are free with a 24 hour entrance ticket.

NB The dirt roads in this area are notoriously steep, and will be almost impossible after prolonged rain.

Lanquin to Coban, 56km – The climb up to the junction at Pajal will be hard work, although the scenery is stunning and changes throughout the climb. Obviously this is one to do early or take advantage of the morning buses.

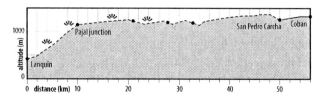

Onwards the road is being improved rapidly, which is good for the reduction in dust, bad for the speed that vehicles will be able to travel at. There are some incredible views through the pine trees, as the road gently climbs passing some small settlements with shops. There are a few small hills before the road climbs into richer vegetation and winds around steep sided outcrops for a few km, before dropping into **San Pedro Carcha.**

Often overlooked, this is the locals' town servicing a wide area of rural Alta Verapaz, there are some excellent markets, and many street traders. The town is almost completely surrounded by a bow in the river, and the old bridge is a nice entrance on the Lanquin side. If on a tight budget it's generally cheaper for accommodation than Coban.

It's a short 6km to Coban, on paved roads, predominately climbing then dropping slightly.

Coban

This coffee capital is past it's best, but still caters well for passing tourists. Banking, internet and other essential facilities, are all within walking distance of the central plaza. There are budget accommodations near the market, down steep streets below the cathedral. Other options are on the plaza, or in the streets around. The area around Coban is famous for producing excellent coffee and cardamom, valuable export crops. The climate is temperate and moist, meaning plenty of drizzle and a heavy mist, although the sun does emerge most days.

Side trips

San Pedro Carcha – It's worth a visit, the markets are excellent, and the town itself is almost completely surrounded by a bow in a river, with nice old bridges, particularly on the road toward Lanquin.

San Juan Chamelco – This small town is only 8 km on paved road from Coban, and a nice quiet ride if needing to stretch your legs. There is no accommodation, although several places to eat and relax. Onward unresearched routes go to San Pedro Carcha and Tactic.
Nearby is the much advertised ranch of San Jeronimos, with organic food and activities.

The journey from **Coban to Fray Bartolome de las Casas** is stunning, and relatively easy this way round, it could be worth doing in day, stopping over in Fray Bartoleme the night and getting the bus back the following day. The route is described in reverse on pg??

Coban to El Estor 200km – This route is all the more pleasant being almost entirely flat or downhill, but it also passes through a big variety of forested scenery, is off the tourist trail and the prettiest way to get from the highlands to the Caribbean.

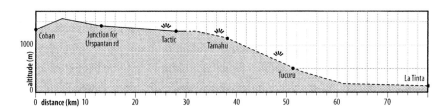

The route to Tactic is straight forward on the road toward the capital, just climb gently for a few km out of Coban then it's downhill all the way. The road can be busy (particularly watch out for the old Greyhound buses) and the traffic fast, although there is plenty of space for cycling.

Tactic is a pleasant place to spend the night, with a few places to stay. From the town, head south, the dirt road branches left off the highway after a couple of km. It's flat at first, then descends, steeply in places, through beautiful thick forest, with a few isolated farms and ranches.

Tamahu and Tucuru are pleasant villages with a shop or two, after Tucuru the road starts to flatten out, and the forest gives way to more farmland. However, La Tinta further on in the agricultural plains is not a particularly nice place to get stuck in.

Teleman is scruffy but pleasant, and a good place to break the journey after 100km, there are a couple lodgings available. The beautiful side trip into the mountains to Senahu is worth considering (see below).

Onwards to Panzos and El Estor, the road can be very dusty and unpleasant when the occasional vehicle passes, and the scenery can get a little montonous, being mainly ranchland. However, there are some interesting river crossings, and the road occasionally climbs foothills, giving good views over the plains below.

There are a couple of buses from Coban to El Estor and occasional pick-ups and trucks, if wanting to skip the later sections.

☞ see p.90 for **El Estor**

Teleman to Senahu, 30km – It's a beautiful journey, although with two climbs (450m and 800m) and there are no opportunities for supplies and water.

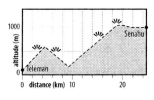

The views from the first climb are amazing north and south, from the second climb the views south are again amazing through the coffee plantations. From where the road meanders around the mountain side, before entering the beautiful valleys nearer Senahu. It's easy to understand why the topography and local resistance meant the Conquistadors couldn't beat these people with force.

There are one or two buses a day and occasional trucks from Teleman.

Senahu

Hidden in the mountains, it has an almost magical feel to it. There's a small hillock to the SE which is a cemetery with a observatory at the top for a nice view of the town. Several places sell food, and a small permanent market has basic supplies. For accommodation there is a mix of options from the most basic hospedaje, to a pleasant hotel on the plaza.

This area is reputed to be one of the best for the possibility of seeing Quetzals, a good eye in the early morning is needed.

The ITMB map doesn't show all the routes in these mountains

SIDE TRIP
Take the dirt road west, up the very steep hill behind the town, for routes toward the Chijolom ruins, and other beautiful valleys. Ask locally for advice, on cycling and walking possibilities, the Hotel in the plaza is one source worth trying for information. It's worth learning a few words of Kekchi, as some people can't or choose not to speak Spanish.

Asking someone to draw a map can bring out peoples artistic side!

Senahu to Semuc Champey (about 60km) – *NB Some off-roading skills required.*
A dream of a journey, though not without some hard pedalling.
    Take a left turn (right goes to Teleman) at the junction on the eastern edge of town, and climb through the forest for 5 km. The road then descends, into beautiful pastureland, and passes a large farm on the left. Continuing, there are several peaceful villages, farmland and forest. At the next two junctions turn left, the first is signed right to Cabahon (the long way round!), the second, after a long and very beautiful descent through forest, is obvious, there's a normally a chain across this turning to a farm. From this point the road undulates through Cardomom, coffee, and forest. The next right turn is the correct route, but it's worth continuing for the 4km to the finca Volcan, even though the road goes no further, as the views are unforgettable.
The ITMB map shows this route
    When you've seen enough, go back to the previous junction, and prepare for a very steep descent with lots of loose stone . If not confident in this, it's better to walk. At the base, turn left through a small settlement, the track follows the valley all the way to the village of Belen (shops). Shortly afterwards is a bridge, turn left, the road starts to climb gently on a rough dirt track, through woodland and agricultural communities. A few km on, there is a junction at the edge of pine woodland, bear left and keep climbing. The track shortly emerges into more open land on top of a hill. There are a few small aldeas and isolated houses as the descent begins. This will need some off-roading skills, as it's in an appalling condition, occasionally 4x4s have tried with difficulty.
    At the next T-junction turn right, and still descending, negotiate what's left of the track. This eventually ends up at a bridge, with excellent swimming nearby. The climb (300m) up from the river, is on a better quality dirt road, though is brutally steep in places. From the top, there are a couple of villages, and two turnings as the road descends – the first comes down from the left,

keep going straight, the second branches off to the right, head left. Then it's almost all downhill for the last few km.

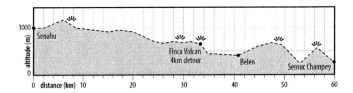

Semuc Champey
A ticket to these cascades lasts for 24hours, and includes camping or covered hammock slinging next to the pools. There is also hostel 2km away on the Lanquin road. It does get very crowded at weekends and holidays, but there's a lot of space and it can make it more fun.

To Lanquin, is a short 10km, but with a steep climb of 400m. From the car park descend to the bridge, the road then climbs steeply over a ridge, drops briefly, then climbs steadily to a pass, with good views.
☞ see p.84 for **Lanquin**

Coban to Urspantan and onto the Ixil Triangle
☞ see p.60 for a description of this route in reverse.

Coban–Guatemala City/Antigua
There is a choice of two routes to the capital:
1) The main highway to the Capital is beautiful, from Coban the road has been much improved, and there is plenty of space for cycling. However, it's worth taking a bus from El Rancho junction, as the Caribbean highway is very busy, narrow and basically dangerous.
NB Be wary of speeding buses.
The highway climbs over the coffee covered mountains before following a valley down to Tactic. For the next 50km to the junction La Cumbre the route passes through some stunning mountain scenery and excellent views of the Sierra de Minas. There are occasional comedors and shops, although the distances varies considerably between them. The road climbs and falls regularly, around the mountains passing the **Biotopo Mario Dary Quetzal reserve**.

There are a couple of places to stay nearby, although neither are budget options and unfortunately camping is no longer allowed in the reserve. There are a couple of well marked trails climbing through the forest, although the chances of actually seeing a quetzal are small.

Onwards the road climbs to the highpoint at La Cumbre, and it's an excellent downhill for almost all the 48km to El Rancho junction, this is worth doing with time to spare even if taking a bus on the rest of the journey. The pine clad mountain sides gradually giving way to hot semi-desert scenery with cactus and scrub, the last few km ride across the Motugua valley will be hot. There are very regular buses from El Rancho to the capital or the Caribbean coast.
2) Via Rabinal on the old road
NB Towards the end of the dry season the landscapes on this route can look barren.
Coban to Salama – The straight forward option is to Tactic, climb up towards Pantin and turn off right on the unresearched cut through to Salama after (57km).

The more interesting option (88km) is taking a bus or cycling to the La Cumbre junction, before enjoying the 14km downhill (nearly) all the way to **Salama.** This small dusty town is set in plains surrounded by mountains, there are busy permenant markets, and little else to do,

but wander round them. Basic accommodation is available.
Salama to Rabinal, 19km – The road climbs through the dry plains and over a small ridge
before descending to San Miguel Chicaj. It's then a long climb up the side of the mountains,
this area is very arid at the end of the dry season, but the views are superb. From the pass
there's a steep winding descent into the valley of Rabinal.

Rabinal

This traditional town is a nice place to stop for the night, it has a couple of decent and cheap
hospedajes. There is a permenant market in the plaza, and numerous street food venders.
Bicycles are popular, it's interesting to note the number of women cycling about in the town!
   A road continues to Cubulco (regular buses and pickups), from where there is a route
across the mountains to **Joyabaj** (☞ see p.61), check locally for track conditions, this is an old
route that has only been part researched and may be beyond a bike!

Rabinal to Guatemala city about 100km – This route is the old highway to the capital, and is
very beautiful, although there are two big climbs, with long distances between refreshments
possibilities and shops. El Chol is the only place with official accommodations.
There are one or two buses a day on this route, it takes at least 5 hours and usually more, to
get to the Capital.
   From Rabinal, it's a solid 1000+m climb up to the pass, although the dusty road is well graded.
The scenery change, from dry land to mixed wooded hillsides is interesting, and the views
behind spectacular. The drop down into El Chol is steeper, but the views are just as beautiful.

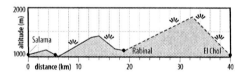

El Chol is a small, pleasant town, with a busy market square and a quaint, basic hospedaje.
There are some nice walks in the area.

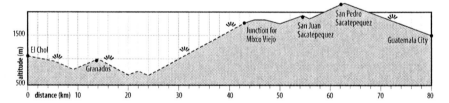

Onwards, the road is very hilly, passing a couple of villages and isolated farms, whilst gradually
descending into the forested Motagua basin. The heat can be stifling, and there are only one
or two places for refreshments near the valley bottom. The climb out of this valley is long and
hard, the gradients are not too steep, but the heat will take it's toll. The dryland forest gradually
changes to pine woodland eventually joining the route from Mixco Viejo at the top, it's then a
paved road all the way to the capital.
   There's a winding descent into a forested valley, then a undulating climb up the other side
to San Juan Sacatepequez, and another steady 6km climb to San Pedro Sacatepequez.

The Caribbean coast

Rio Dulce AKA El Relleno
This town is functional rather than pretty, but the views from the top of the bridge make it special and the surrounding lakeside is a nice place to relax. Lago Izabal is the playground of the Guatemalan rich, the contrasts of wealth couldn't be greater.

There are a few places to stay, a pleasant budget option is the backpacker's lodge just over the straits on the other side of the bridge.

SIDE TRIP
Rio Dulce to Livingston – there are launches to Livingston, these have radically risen in price over the previous years, but it is still a unique trip. If organised by a group, it's possible to go via the Manatee sanctuary, but all pass through the magnificent gorges of the Rio Dulce, before the channel widens out nearer Livingston. Taking a bike may be as much as double the normal price, it will depend how small you can make your bike.

Livingston
This town is home to perhaps the only musically gifted peoples in Guatemala. The Garifuna use Reggae, ska, and bass mixed in unique styles, there are regular live music nights. The food is likewise very different to the latin cuisine. A bike is a good way to get around, although everything is within walking distance. There are a range of accomodations, from hammock slinging to rooms.

From Livingston to Puerto Barrios, there are regular scheduled boats, several fast launches, and a slower cargo boat, which is also cheaper for transporting a bike.

NB There have been regular traveller stories of robbery and theft on the nearby beaches, ask locally for up-to-date information.

90

Rio Dulce to El Estor, 50km – The paved part of this road climbs and falls around foothills for 20km and is then flatter. It is gradually being improved, the following 30km will be paved in the next couple of years. The scenery is mostly ranchland, with good views across the plains and lake. There are very few opportunities for refreshment and it can get very hot during the day, although there is a little shade from trees along the roadside.

Halfway, the thermal springs at finca El Paraiso are worth stopping off for, there is a small admission charge. It's possible to stay nearby on the lakeside in cabanas, although it works out much cheaper for a group.

The dusty road continues along the base of the foothills, through ranchland and a few small villages until the **Canyon el Boqueron**, 5km before El Estor. This is definitely worth making time for, although it could be done as a day trip from El Estor. There are boats and canoes for hire to take people the twenty minutes upstream into the canyon, and it is impressive, dawn and dusk are good times to see the bats and birds. Swimming and walking against the flow, is a slightly more strenuous way of exploring. Discreet camping or hammock slinging nearby is possible.

El Estor
This lakeside town is growing rapidly thanks to the new road to Rio Dulce. There are a few places to stay around the plaza or along the waterfront. The markets are lively, and the views across the lake fantastic especially at dawn. This town is potentially a new tourist/adventure centre in the making, and already attracts many locals for the holidays.

El Estor to Rio Dulce 50km – See the reverse route description on the previous page
Try to leave early in order to see the Canyon El Boqueron at dawn, and to avoid the midday
heat, which can be sapping.
NB For the last 20 km there are no places for water or food.

Rio Dulce to Pto Barrios by road, 85km – This is an unremarkable trip. Head south across the
lakeside plains, Benque is pleasant enough for a food or drink stop, before a climb over the
hills to La Rudioso, there are coconut milk sellers at the top if needing a refreshing drink.
Onwards, the last 50km are on the Caribbbean highway which is a busy road, so catching a bus
to Puerto Barrios is a reasonable alternative.

Pto Barrios

This is a sleepy port town, it's hey day is now past. Most tourists will only see the route from
the buses to the harbour (For Livingston and Punta Gorda). However, the covered markets are
lively, and the town is easy to negotiate on bike, there are several places to stay near the market.
Fast launches and a slower cargo boat service the route to Livingston, the slower boat is
the easiest and cheapest for taking a bike.

Pto Barrios to Guatemala city to Pto Barrios, 85km – This is an easy road for which to
recommend taking a bus, it's very busy with heavy traffic and has little space for cycling on
several sections. However the **Quirigua ruins** after 92km, are a worthwhile side trip.
They are special for having a much richer artistry in their carved stone stelae, than other
ruins in Guatemala. They are on a smaller scale than the Copan ruins in Honduras, but have a
similar history. The site is surrounded by a couple of acres of lush forest, in a sea of banana
plantations. The nearby town of Quirigua has basic accommodations.
There's an interesting ride to the ruins along the disused train tracks at the back of Quirigua
town, although the bridges need taking carefully. These tracks cross the road close to the ruins,
after another km or two. One day it would be nice to dream of a cycle track along these
disused tracks from the capital to the coast!

91

Puerto Barrios to Omoa (Honduras) 80km – There are 13km of busy main road to Entre Rios,
which are tolerable due to the space at the roadside. Turn right at the edge of this settlement,
passing over a small ridge, there are a couple of shops and comedors in this part of town. The
road then meanders through the plains to the Guatemalan immigration formalities after about
10km.
The next part of this route is not included on ITMB map(s)
A new paved road continues through the banana plantations to the Honduran border at
Corinto. crossing the Rio Motagua. There are occasional settlements for the seasonal workers,
which have basic shops and comedors.
*NB There is aerial crop spraying of the banana plantations, apparently this happens once a
month or so, by all reports they are indiscriminate.*
There is little shade across the plains, so it's worth starting early. As the mountains become
larger in the distance, the Honduran border approaches. Immigration is in Corinto, surrounded
by a few money changers, so it's difficult to miss. Onwards to Omoa the dirt road traces the
edge of foothills, with views overlooking the ranchland plains, and some occasional shade.
There are a few dusty settlements, lush vegetation, more ranches, further on there are views of
the sea as the route approaches Omoa. This road is due for improvement.
☞ see p.116 for **Omoa**

HONDURAS

> *If planning a trip to Honduras only to visit the Copan ruins, it may be a good compromise to consider going to the Quirigua ruins, between Zacapa and Puerto Barrios in Guatemala instead. The beautiful stelae are similar, and the side trip to Copan is a long detour.*

Customs and immigration – For most nationalities entering for up to 90 days, by filling out a simple tourist card, should be no problem. There are different entrance and exit taxes depending on where a border is being crossed, although neither is excessive, ask for a receipt if concerned, arguing goes down very badly.

People – The mestizo population dominates and the culture is more Americanised than Guatemala. Of the indigenous groups the **Lenca** are an interesting people, apparently they were never given to empire building, like the Mayans or Aztecs, and formed semi-autonomous communities. This made them a real headache for the invading Spanish, who were used to controlling unruly people by knocking out their leader. A warrior called Lempira eventually united the Lenca to fight, and was honoured by becoming the unit of currency. The people live in the mountains from Gracias to Marcala.

There are smaller groups of indigenous peoples near Yoro and La Mosquita and are many black Garifuna commmunities along the coast and on the islands.

Money and costs – The currency is Lempiras, named after a national hero. Honduras is the cheapest country covered in this guide.

Roads – The road network between large towns and cities is in good condition, and there's normally plenty of space for cycling and not much traffic. Whilst many of the cross country dirt roads are being improved, it's still possible to cross the country on tracks and unpaved roads. It is a true cyclists paradise.

Alternative transport – The buses are mostly old American school buses like Guatemala, however they don't go to such lengths to decorate them. On the longer routes there are larger more luxorious models. Pick-ups are used everywhere in country areas, and very useful for occasional lifts.

General tips and observations

- The good quality local coffee is used and enjoyed everywhere, by almost everyone. The highlands from Copan to Marcala and Comayagua are the main coffee growing areas.
- It's possible to get a reasonable map from Texaco stations. Or in the Capital at the tourist office (3rd floor in the Lloyds TSB building, near the American embassy), which is free.
- There is good quality market food and the usual beans and rice etc, but the street food selection is not as good as other countries
- There are more pretty tiled roofs, and some areas of deforestation due to the wood needed to make them.
- Government park and ruins fees are similar prices to Mexico and Guatemala, Some good-natured haggling can work at the less visited sites, as there are different prices for locals.

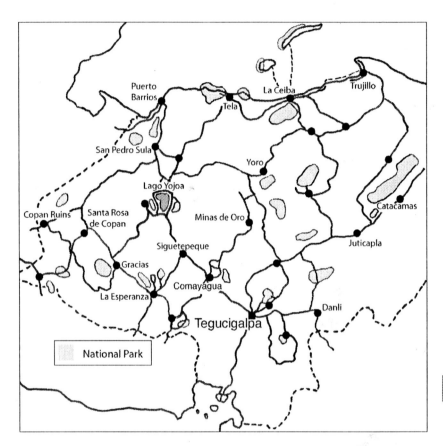

Puerto Barrios
La Ceiba
Trujillo
Tela
San Pedro Sula
Yoro
Lago Yojoa
Catacamas
Copan Ruins
Santa Rosa de Copan
Minas de Oro
Siguetepeque
Juticalpa
Gracias
Comayagua
La Esperanza
Danli
Tegucigalpa

National Park

- Honduras is fortunate in not being badly afflicted by earthquakes.
- There are not many tourists, most are concentrated around the 'honey pots' of Copan and the Bay islands.
- *The ITMB map of Honduras, has several old roads marked that are now little more than footpaths, they are noted in the text*

Olancho reputation

The department of Olancho has a gained a bad reputation over the last few years, mainly for theft and robbery. There certainly is a wild west feel in places, but the lawlessness has been exaggerated. If unsure ask locally for the current situation before embarking on a route. The diverse natural beauty of the area is worth making the effort to visit.

Cycling Highlights

- The backroads between Cucuyagua and Gracias (via Belen Gualcho) in the highlands
- The climb from Marcala to Goajiquiro and descent to San Pedro Tutule.
- The ride from Comayagua via Las Minas de Oro to Yoro.
- La Union to Olanchito, is remote, but a stunning ride on mountain roads.

Example of 2 week cycling tour route around Tegucigalpa
Tegucigalpa-Valle de Angeles-Talanga-Minas De Oro-Comayagua-bus side trip to Lago Yojoa -
La Esperanza-Marcala-Goajiquiro-La Paz-Tegucigalpa

The highlands

El Florido to Copan Ruins, 12km – Try not to change any money until reaching the town of
Copan Ruinas, as the rates at the border are poor. Once clear of immigration, the paved road
climbs through cleared woodland, it can be steep in places. There are some good views from a
short undulating section at the top and then a long downhill toward Copan Ruinas. The town
centre is signed from the road, turn left opposite the butterfly house, this cuts through the
back of town on cobbles to the markets and plaza.

Copan Ruinas
This pretty colonial town has been given a make over in the last few years, and it's a pleasant
place to stay and relax for a couple of days. There are a couple of banks and a mix of
accommodation and comedors to suit most budgets. The tourist office is on the steep slope
down from the plaza, and good for picking up a copy of the useful *Honduras Tips* magazine.
New excursions are springing up all the time locally, from caving and tubing to horseriding.

The Copan ruins
These Mayan ruins are something special. There is a finer degree of carving in the working of
the stelae, probably due in part to a different quality of available stone, but new theories have
suggested that the indigenous Lenca of Honduras may have had an influence as well. The
entrance fee is only a few dollars and the ruins are worth a few hours. To get there walk or
cycle a couple of km from town, on the road to San Pedro Sula, there's also an excellent
museum on the same site.

    A couple of km further on the right there are more (slightly less impressive) ruins, footpaths
also lead down to the river. These are much less visited by tourists, if wanting to get away from
the crowds.

Copan Ruinas to Cucuyagua (Cross country) about 70km – This route is not easy,
particularly when carrying panniers etc. However it does offer excellent views and scenery, on
quiet dirt roads and tracks.
The ITMB map should not be relied on for navigation on this route

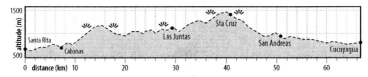

There is no official accommodation en route, but there are a couple of basic hopedajaes in
Cucuyagua, to get there in one day would mean leaving very early!! Secure camping with
permission or asking to pay for a room in one of the settlements in between are the other
options.
    From Copan Ruinas, take the main road for a few km to Santa Rita and turn right into this
old village. Crossing over the river bridge, a dirt road follows the the river valley up to Cabanas.

This is a pleasant quiet community with a few shops and a nice plaza. Turn left on the far side of the plaza, the road shortly fords a river, with a wire rope and clapper footbridge, if the water is too deep. This is where the real climbing starts, the track is usually in good condition, although has a couple of short muddy sections and some steeper granny gear work outs. The vegetation gradually changes with altitude into coffee and banana growing areas, with good views back down the valley. Nearer the top there is more pine woodland and the road flattens out along a ridge, again with good views.

The descent toward **Rio Negras**, is well graded and for the last km's follows a river down to the village. There is a shop for basic supplies, it will be the last for a while! Take the turning left by the shop, (ask for the road to Las Juntas or Santa Cruz if unsure), and cross the river on the wire rope and clapper bridge. This rough track climbs steeply for a couple of km passing several houses, but levels out with great views, there are several rivers to cross with short but steep climbs up the other side

NB The track has some short but deep muddy sections after rain.

Eventually this track reaches the settlement of **Las Juntas**, which is very spread out, and has a basic comedor and a couple of shops. Shortly after is the last river crossing, and the road starts to climb up toward the mountain pass, steeply in places. There's a beautiful section along a ridge, after which is junction left (this eventually leads back down to the La Entrada paved road), keep going straight on and climb the last few km up through the small settlements of Platonares and Ladrillo. The village of **Santa Cruz**, is a short drop on the other side of the pass, and has a couple of shops. It is a lovely village, with many old but dishevelled buildings and offers good views There are no official accommodations, although asking for a room is a possibility.

The descent continues eventually passing San Miguel, on the edge of a massive gold mine. Onwards there may be some heavier mining traffic, the road winds around the edge of the spoil mound, before crossing a river and climbing over a pretty pine forested ridge. Near the top there's a junction (left) to San Augustin, keep going straight and drop through the forest into the modern settlement of San Andres. This village is mainly a workers compound, with a couple of places to eat, although no accommodation. There are some thermal springs not far away, although it's difficult to actually bathe in them. Several paths lead down into the valley, and the sulphurous fumes should be visible a little further up the river.

To Cucuyagua, the road drops down and crosses a bridge, with a short climb up the other side. This is repeated several times as the road crosses the undulating plain, passing close to the traditional villages of El Corpus and La Union. The road comes out on the highway between Nuevo Octepeque and Santa Rosa De Copan, turn left and cross the bridge to **Cucuyagua** which is an unassuming staging post with a bank and basic hospedaje if needed.

☞ see p.97 for the routes to **Belen Gualcho** and **Santa Rosa**

Copan Ruinas to La Entrada 53km – A good quality paved road which is a relatively quiet at present, although as cross border trade is increasesing it will have more heavy traffic. The scenery is pleasant varying often from semi-forested hills to open ranch land. The terrain whilst hilly is not too severe, there is one main climb with good views, and several villages en route for supplies and water.

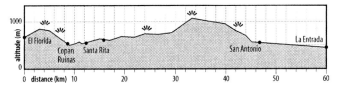

Santa Rita is a pleasant old settlement, a few km from Copan, there are also some more touristy water parks and attractions on the way.

La Entrada – is a functional but uninteresting place to pass through on the way to somewhere else. There are accommodations if needed.

La Entrada to San Pedro Sula, 118km – The route is uncycled, but twice travelled. It follows the descending Ulua river, although the road climbs over many hills and side valleys. The scenery is very green and beautiful, and there are good views over to the mountains in the east. There are no accommodations on the route until much closer to the city, which makes this potentially a long day in the saddle.
The turning to the **Cusco National park** is signed from Cofradia. It's another 35km on a dirt road to the park entrance. This is unresearched, but it's reputed to be a good place to see Quetzals, with potentially good cycling on old logging tracks and footpaths into the mountains.
    As the city gets closer so the road gets much busier, passing factories, and larger communities, it also gets hotter.

La Entrada to Santa Rosa de Copan, 37km – This road climbs significantly, crossing a couple of valleys on the way, but gives some wonderful mountain views. There is some heavy traffic, but plenty of space for cycling safely. It's worth stocking up in La Entrada as there are only one or two small shophuts on the way.

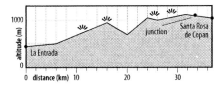

If wanting to go straight to **Gracias** (☞ see p.100), the junction is on the left, on the ridge before the the 2km descent to **Santa Rosa**, see p.99

Esquipulas to Nueva Octepeque, 28km – This route into Honduras is interesting as after Neuva Octepeque there are some big climbs through beautiful countryside, it's not so popular with tourists, as it misses out the Copan ruins.
    There's an undulating climb up to the Guatemalan customs point (the money changers offer

poor rates at the border) and then a 1km descent to Honduran immigration. Onwards is a long steady descent through sparse pine woodland with isolated farmsteads. At the bottom is a river crossing, before a gentle climb up to Nueva Octepeque.

Nueva Octepeque – There are banks for changing money, hospedajes and small markets for supplies in this small town, although there is little else to detain a visitor.

The village of Old Octepeque is a few km away down the road toward El Salvador, from where there are tracks to the river. An old clapper bridge leads to a hamlet and nice places to camp on the other side (ask permission).

Neuva Octepeque to Santa Rosa de Copan, 78km – This would be a hard days hard ride. There are two big climbs, but both give exceptional views as compensation.

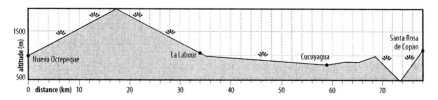

NB Sometimes the police make immigration checks on the edge of Neuva Octepeque.

The first climb is 15km long, but has a steady gradient as it winds around the sides of the mountains, passing a few basic places for supplies, and a couple of comedors. The pass cuts through a small but atmospheric reserve of cloud forest, it can be covered in mist! and the temperature drops considerably. Descending the other side, local vegetable and fruit sellers line the road, further down, La Labor with shops and comedors is the first roadside settlement reached of any size. Continuing, the road undulates, but is gently descending, along a beautiful valley of dry land scenery for 27km to **Cucuyagua**.

This is an important trading centre for a wide rural area, having a range of shops for supplies as well as a small bank and hospedaje if needed. There are interesting side routes south to Corquin and Belen Gualcho, and north to Santa Cruz, from this small town (see below).

Onwards the scenery is mostly agricultural, the road starts to climb again for few km before a big descent with amazing views into a deep valley below. The bigger ascent up the other side, has several switchbacks, although the road remains well graded. **Santa Rosa de Copan** is just over the other side of the pass. ☞ see p.99

97

Cucuyagua–Corquin–Belen Gualcho

A visit to these pretty colonial settlements is well worth the effort, as they still retain the old charm, and the surrounding mountains and countryside are beautiful.

Cucuyagua to Corquin, 12km – There's a good paved road to Corquin, it undulates gently over the dry agricultural plains for a few km, before passing by the old village of San Pedro (shops). It then drops to cross a river before climbing over a small ridge to Corquin.

Corquin

This pleasant colonial town is perfect to wander around, as the old cobbles make for slow cycling. There are two distinct parts to it, seperated by a river. Most miss the older part of town, passing the newer plaza on the way to Belen Gualcho. On the other side of the river, there's a

rough cobbled street up to a plaza, bank and a few more shops. The old buildings are generally in good condition and give the place nice atmosphere. There are a couple of places to stay, one basic option and the other more comfortable.

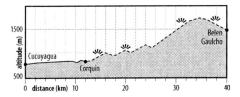

Corquin to Belen Gualcho, 30km – This is a tough, but beautiful climb, the gradients are ok with only a couple of steeper sections, and the views fantastic, clouds permitting.

For the first 15km, the well made dirt road climbs then undulates, climbs then dips etc, passing a couple of settlements, until starting to climb more steadily. The views are good with coffee, bananas, eucalyptus and pines predominating on the roadside. There is often mist and cloud nearer the top of the climb where the road levels out for a couple of km, before starting to drop toward Belen Gaulcho, there are a few turnoffs, but follow the roads to the right on descent and after another few km the beginnings of civilisation will appear.
If tired, the last bus is at 3pm, there are also several pickups until dusk.

Belen Gualcho
This lovely old town is nestled in the mountains, and has a couple of cheap and cheerful places to stay. If possible try to make it for a Sunday market, as the town comes to life.

SIDE TRIPS
There is some excellent walking in the area, ask locally if wanting a guide;
Southeast, toward and up the prominent mountain, Cerro Capitan;
North, to pretty waterfalls (difficult after rain);
South, past the church and graveyard along the side of the valley.

Belen Gualcho to La Campa (and onto Gracias), about 60km – This is a long days ride, but there are places to stay in La Campa and San Sebastian if wanting to travel more slowly. The distances are not great, but climbing (and occasional walking!) in out of all the valleys can be very tiring. The views and scenery are incredible.

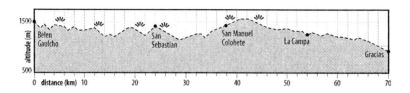

The ride to San Sebastian is hard work, but very beautiful, people still trade with mules on this track. The route goes from the bottom of Belen Gaulcho down to the river, before climbing steeply up the side of the valley into the forest. There are several more climbs and rivers to ford, passing the comunities of Jualaco and Cubite. From the second are great views over the valley. After descending to the river, and crossing the clapper bridge, there's a very stoney climb up to a junction, turning right leads up to San Sebastian after a couple of km, left is the road toward San Manuel.

San Sebastian is a peaceful colonial village with a nice comedor and has great views in almost every direction. It's worth exploring even if tired after the climb!

To San Manuel, is along descent down to a bridge, followed by a long but well graded climb, with great views south There's a small village with a couple of shops on the next flatter section, before a descent, ford and then steepish climb through another valley. San Manuel is half way up the other side, again there's a comedor, but it's a place to pass through, lacking the charm of San Sebastian. The climb up to the pass at Sta Theresa, is steep in places, but with compensation of good views and the knowledge that this is the last hard work. It's almost continually downhill all the way to La Campa, and this is a nice place to stay after long day in the saddle.

La Campa
A pretty, rural settlement in a beautiful setting, there are a couple of basic, but clean hospedajes, both places also serve food. There is a small canyon right next to this pretty village, with good walking opportunities and views of the nearby mountains.

SIDE TRIP
There is potentially excellent off-roading in the coffee growing mountains around the village of Cruz Alto. To get there, take the road to San Miguel and turn left after one km, the track drops down to cross a river, then be prepared for a steepish rough climb, superb all round views from the top, and plenty of tracks to explore.

There is an interesting route to San Juan via Santa Cruz from nearby, that avoids the dusty roads from Gracias.

La Campa to Gracias, the agricultural scenery is less interesting, it's still predominately downhill, although the road crosses several rivers with short climbs afterwards.
☞ see p.100 for **Gracias**

Santa Rosa de Copan
The wealthy colonial part of town, sits on the hill above the road, whilst the modern, including the bus station, is sprawlled along the main road. There are some excellent views from the high points of town over the surrounding countryside and the markets bustle. The town is famous for it's good quality home-grown tobacco and cigars. There are a few places to stay, to suit most budgets, the cheapest is just east of the main plaza.

Santa Rosa de Copan to Gracias, 45km – From Santa Rosa de Copan take the road toward San Pedro Sula, it climbs steadily for a couple of km up to the junction for Gracias. Turning right, this is a quiet paved road, and climbs gently for a couple of km, then there's a big descent, the views through the pine forest into the deep valley are excellent.

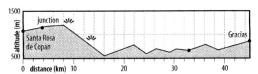

From the bridge at the bottom, there's less shade and gentle undulating climbs over a couple of side valleys, before the road crosses the river again and climbs more steeply up to Gracias. There are few chances for refreshment, except in El Tablon.

Gracias

This old colonial town has a lot of charm and history, it's more laid back than Santa Rosa de Copan although a bit more worn about the edges. There is a mix of places to stay, markets and a variety of comedors, cafes and the obligatory internet facilities. The tourist office is in the centre of the tree lined plaza opposite the church, although at present has limited information.

SIDE TRIPS

The thermal baths (Aguas Thermales), 6km – Very relaxing, they are easily visited either on the way to La Esperanza, or an excursion from Gracias. It's worth spending a night, camping or in a hammoc if possible, as the baths are open late, and an early morning swim is a nice way to greet the day. The small entrance fee covers camping as well. There are several different pools of different temperatures and one large area for swimming. Bringing in food isn't allowed, as basic meals and snacks are available.

Celaque National Park

The mountains in this park have the highest peak in Honduras, and well worth getting off the bike to explore. From Gracias it's about 6km up to the edge of the park, the track is in poor condition in places, but can be cycled. This route is well signed and goes SW out of town, passing through the village of Mejicalpa, and then turns to the right, before climbing through mixed farmland and pine forest. At the park entrance is a centre with basic accommodation for staying overnight. There are signs on where to register and pay the park entrance fee, which has a daily rate.

The park itself is very bio-diverse, although the predominance of pine species until much higher up the slopes disappoints some, the cloud forest starts at about 2200m. The route to the top is reasonably well marked and there are a couple of places to camp en route. The climb (up and down) can be done in a day if very fit and starting at dawn.

There is a large network of dirt roads, tracks and trails around the Celaque mountain range. For large scale maps try the library or the police station.

Gracias to Santa Barbara, about 80km, depending on route – There are several different roads to cross the mountains, the main settlements en route are San Rafael and El Nipper, La Iguala is a short detour. There are many small villages, populated by agricultural workers in the nearby coffee plantations. Looking back, good views can be had of the Celaque NP, the local countryside is very agricultural, and coffee dominates with forest confined to the ridges and

hilltops. There are no official accommodations in the area, so starting early is important, it will be necessary to ask directions often.

☞ see p.115 for **Santa Barbara**

Gracias to San Juan, 52km – This is a beautiful dirt road ride, however it can be very dusty when vehicles pass. It is gradually being improved. The road climbs and falls over a couple of valleys before a long climb up toward Belen. The scenery on this section is beautiful, with excellent views, the prettier sections start after Belen as the road climbs in and out of forested valleys, before a longer climb over a ridge, with a gentle descent into San Juan.

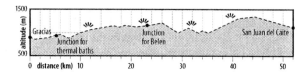

An alternative route to San Juan, which is partially explored, is via La Campa and Sta Cruz. There is a bus a day from Gracias to Sta Cruz at about midday, if wanting to get a good start. From Sta Cruz the road undulates but is mostly downhill. This route avoids the traffic and is through beautiful wooded countryside.

San Juan

A nice place to break the journey and there are couple of basic places to stay and eat. There is a Sunday market, although it's not worth making special plans for. The local peace corps have made a lot of effort to develop a fledging tourist industry, and whilst the town is not particularly special there are several worthwhile excursions. Horses (mules) can easily be rented with a guide for riding into the hills.

SIDE TRIPS

There are also some beautiful circular cycling routes west of San Juan to;

To El Pelon – The treeless hill to the west. It's visible from San Juan, and a popular destination for short mule rides.

To a beautiful small Canyon – Take the dirt road to Erandique, cross the bridge and start climbing for a few km. From the top, the road then descends for a couple of km and splits at a fork, where there's a shop. Take the right turn and follow through the pine forest until reaching a large green area on the left. Turn right again, this track descends to a small river crossing and then bears right. Shortly after comes a field on the right where tiles are made, the canyon is the other side of the field. It's possible to walk around the top on both sides and climb down to the river.

Continuing on, the track climbs, steeply in places, into coffee and banana growing farmland, with excellent views toward San Juan and the Celaque mountains. Descending the other side of this ridge, the next village is Espinal from where there is a short cut back to San Juan. The following village is Cataulaca, and has a shop and a nice cassita/comedor for food if hungry. The road back to San Juan, descends to a river then climbs over a small hill.

San Juan to La Esperanza, 50km – A beautiful route through the forested mountains with little traffic, but it is best started early, due the climbing involved.

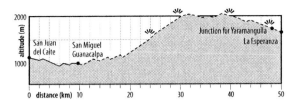

The road is wide and paved to San Miguelito, one of those slightly bizarre presidential gestures. It drops into a valley, with several pan tile manufacturers just off the road. Crossing the riverbridge, the road climbs over a small ridge and down to another bridge, before a short climb up toward the turn off left to San Miguelito. This small rural settlement has a few shops, and is the last chance for supplies before the top of the climb. Once through the village, the mountains start to loom in front.

The first part of the climb is quite steep, and zig-zags up through the pine trees, before dropping back down again to cross a river. The road then follows the valley and the river is crossed twice more, before the long climb starts. The gradients are very reasonable, except on a couple of short sections, the views are mostly obscured by the trees, but they do provide useful shade. Higher up the land has been cleared for agriculture around a few Lenca communities.

At the first obvious junction near the top, there are stunning views westwards, and a waterpoint at the side of the road. Onwards the road climbs and falls around the side of the mountain, before emerging into more open farmland, and begins the long descent toward La Esperanza. Go straight on at the only junction with another dirt highway, it's another couple of km into town, take care as this road is often badly rutted.

La Esperanza

This is a very pleasant highland town, with many old buildings. The indigenous Lenca people add something unique to this whole area. There are a few cheap, basic accommodations and a couple of hotels. The lively markets are full of excellent local vegetables, and there's a good variety of street food. The Catholic church do sometimes broadcast surreal music very loudly on Sunday mornings.

The ITMB map should not be relied on for exploration in this area.
The police station has a big large scale map of the local area, that they may let you look at, if you can explain what you want to do!
The area north west of town has some excellent off-roading, with tracks and trails to explore.

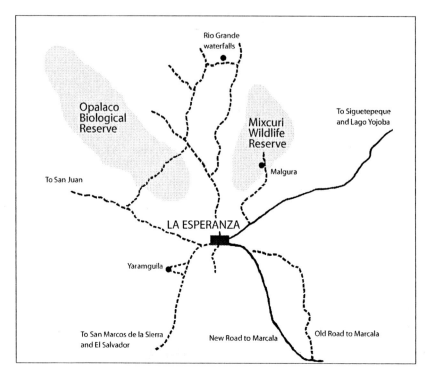

SIDETRIPS
Yaramanguila
The ride up to this town retraces the climb toward Gracias, before branching left after 3km. It's a long steady climb, but not too taxing. The road passes through a small settlement and a couple of km later there is a turning right to the town. This road rises briefly and there's a pleasant descent the rest of the way.

This is a Lenca community, and pleasant enough, although there's not much of interest. Ask locally for directions to nearby waterfalls.

Malguara and the bioreserve
The old road to Malguara as marked on the ITMB map, is in a terrible state, and would be a challenging ride for most off-roaders. The route starts by turning off the dirt road toward the Rio Grand waterfalls (see below) There are several unmarked tracks in this area leading off in many directions, although it would be difficult to get completely lost.

The newer road to Malguara, branches off from the highway to Siguetepeque after a few km. The turning is not signed. The road climbs and falls over several ridges and valleys, there are good views and nice forest/ farmland scenery. It can be rough going in places, with some short, steep sections.

A sensible alternative might be to take the bus up to El Rodeo, from where it's predominately downhill cycling back to town.

Rio Grande waterfalls, 40km round trip

The road heads north from the corner of a football pitch, 2 blocks east of the main road to Gracias (ask for the road to San Nicholas). There's a steady climb, for a few km, although the dirt road is quiet and has pleasant forest scenery. At the first obvious fork, bear right, it should be marked. Shortly after, the road passes the small lake of Chiligatoro on the right, and starts to descend. Keep going for several km until reaching the village of Rio Grande. There's a football pitch, and a shop by the turning left to the waterfalls. It's another 1.5km descent, and then the way is marked from the road, for another 400m. The waterfalls have a 100m+ drop and are quite impressive. The grassy area above them is perfect for camping, although the local children may be a little curious.

Coming back, either the same way or continue, crossing over the Rio Grande, and climb up to a junction. Turn left, and continue for another few km, turning left at the next junction as well. The road has short steep climbs in places, but offers good views, passing several small settlements and farms. At the next junction on a plain, turn left again, and pass through a small village. There's another short climb before the road descends to a junction (the first fork encountered on the way out), it's then a nice downhill to La Esperanza.

San Marcos de la Sierra 30km one-way

This is a beautiful ride to make one way, and then get a lift on the way back.

Take the road as for Yaramguila, but don't turn off. The road undulates through the pine forest then starts to descend, snaking around the sides of the mountains. The views are incredible, the temperatures start to climb, and the forest starts to thin out. The narrow road is in poor condition in places, with a lot of loose stone, although it is being steadily improved.

San Marcos has a few comedors and shops, with great views over countryside below. Getting a lift back to La Esperanza shouldn't be too difficult, as all traffic seems to stop in the village, there are occasional buses and many pick-ups.

La Esperanza to Siguetepeque, 60km – This good quality road makes a change from the bumpy journey over the mountains from San Juan, however there are a few pot holes to watch out for on the speedy descents. There is little shade on this route, although a few trees provide some cover on the climb up from Jesus de Otoro.

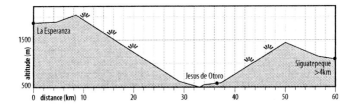

After cycling out of the plains around La Esperanza, there is a short climb for a few km before a very fast downhill into a dry valley basin. On a clear day the views are amazing and temperatures rise quickly. There are only one or two places for supplies or refreshment, until Jesus de Otoro, which is a little nicer than it seems from the road, there are a few shops, a shady plaza and comedors in the market.

The climb up the other side of the valley is long, but well graded and has good views. There are a few comedors, shops and fruit sellers, although little shade. The pass is a few km behind the edge of the valley, and doesn't offer great vistas. The road then drops steadily down

toward Siguetepeque, looping across the plains. Cross the intercity highway and bear right, the
town is a couple of km along a straight road.
Siguetepeque – Is modern, functional, and pleasant, but it doesn't have great deal to interest
travellers. A good place if wanting a meal break.

Siguetepeque to Lago de Yojoa, 40km – This is a straight forward ride on the main intercity
route. It can be busy, but there is enough space for cycling at the side of road.

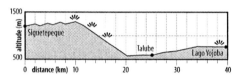

There's a gentle undulating climb for a 12 km, to the km130 sign, with several fruit sellers near
the highest point. As the road drops into the Taulabe valley the views are spectacular. A large
cave system is open for guided tours near this settlement. Onwards there's a steady and gentle
climb, through a few small settlements all the way up to the lake.

La Esperanza to La Marcala, 36km – The dirt track route through the forest is beautiful, make
sure to take the old road, there is new paved road being constructed which will be completed
to La Esperanza in 2005.

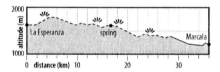

From La Esperanza, head East out of town along a 4-lane road. At the end of the plain, the
dirt road climbs over a ridge with a couple of farmsteads, and then quickly disappears into
thick pine forest. There are one or two farms, but otherwise it can feel quite remote. There are 3
dips to climb out of on the way down, then the road levels briefly and there is a spring on the
side of the road. It then starts to descend more steadily, with occasional excellent views
through the trees, especially nearing sunset.

After 15km or so the forest opens out into a hilly plain with a few Lenca settlements. The
dirt road joins the new highway and begins a long smooth descent, the last few km are more
or less level. Turn right at the junction at the end, there's a short climb over a ridge before
dropping into Marcala.

La Marcala
An important trading post for a large rural area and it's a pleasant place to spend a night, there
are a couple of cheap hospedajes and a hotel for accommodation. Good internet facilities, a
couple of banks and some large covered markets, should cover most needs.

Local side trips to nearby Lenca communities, can be arranged through a couple called
Nayo and Vinda, who live near San Jose, they are well known, and locals can offer directions to
where they can be found.
☞ see p.108 for routes to **San Jose** and onto **La Paz**

105

La Marcala to Goajiquiro, about 65km – For a real insight into Lenca culture with stunning mountain scenery and views, this detour is worth making time for.
The ITMB map should not be reled on for navigation on this route

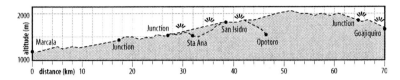

Head south out of Marcala, toward Yarula, the road from is well graded and climbs steadily at first, then there are a few flatter sections and hollows. Followed by more steady climbing through Milpa and woodland. There are several small settlements on this road, with a few small shops.

After about 12km, there's a steep turning left, it's unmarked so if in doubt ask for the way to Opotoro. This road climbs in steps and passes through several farming communities, after another 10km there's a Y-junction, with a shop in the middle:

Right – after climbing over ridge for 5km this route reaches Santa Ana, a small village with a shop and good views. There's an alternative route on rough tracks and trails from Santa Ana that eventually rejoins the Opotoro road near San Isidro. However there are too many turnoffs and junctions to describe, so being confident enough to ask directions (to San Isidro) is essential;
Left – Is the direct route to Opotoro and Goajiquiro. The road continues to climb through the farmland/woodland, passing through Santiago and other smaller communities.

From San Isidro the gradients get kinder as the road follows the ridge of the mountains, there's more forest, and many flowers.

At the next main junction is the road to Opotoro this road drops down steadily for 4-5km through the forest, although the last 0.5km is much steeper. In the village itself is a nice comedor, and a few shops, although the climb back up to the Goajiquiro road is tough after a lot of food.

Back at the junction the road continues climbing, there are occasional settlements, but the distances between them gets longer. There is no easily definable peak, although the section through the cloud forest seems to be as high as it gets. Eventually the road starts an undulating descent, there are a few junctions but continue straight on. Lower down as the road starts to bend round to the right, there's a bigger junction, go straight on (left is to San Pedro Tutule), at the next junction keep right (left goes to San Jose). Follow this road as it seems to bend back on itself, climbing briefly, before descending more steeply around the side of the mountain. There are a couple more turnings, but the main route is obvious.

A less energetic alternative is to take one of the two buses from La Paz or San Pedro Tutule to Goajiquiro, and cycle from there.

Goajiquiro
This Lenca commmunity is a friendly place to stay, there's a basic hospedaje (ask locally for the person with the key) and a couple of comedors. The views over the mountains and valleys below are superb, and apparently(!) it rarely gets cloudy.

SIDE TRIPS
A beautiful walk is to Pueblo Nuevo, below Goajiquiro. The track/footpath is sill used for
trading with mules, there and back takes about 3/4 hours. On the way, there are beautiful river
pools to cool off in and an interesting change in scenery. There's a tiny shop, for snacks in
Pueblo Nuevo.
      There are local guides available for walks into the hills, although it's difficult to get lost.

San Jose is another Lenca community, with two co-operatives, one for weaving traditional
fabrics, the other lovely pottery. To get there cycle back up the mountainside, and take the first
obvious right turn. This then descends for several km, first to San Juan, then San Jose. The
pottery Co-op is at the beginning of the village, the textile workshop at the other end, there
are also a couple of old style shops selling a bizarre mixture of things. The ride back has a
couple of steep sections, apparently there are shorter ways of connecting to the San
PedroTutule road, but they involve steeper climbs.

Goajiquiro to San Pedro Tutule/La Paz, about 40km – Climb back up the mountain and turn
right at the second junction (the first is for San Jose). Onwards are 4 more km of gentle
climbing followed by long descent with incredible views. The scenery is mostly of small scale
agricultural communities, lower down is more ranchland and the population is more latinized.
For a bit of exercise there are a couple of ridges and a small valley to climb out of.
      San Pedro Tutule is a peaceful town with a big plaza, there are a variety of shops for
supplies, a few places to eat and a hospedaje if needed.

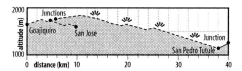

The road to La Paz decends to a river before a short, but steep climb up to the highway. For route descriptions from San PedroTutule to La Paz, see below.

La Marcala to La Paz, 55km – The road is paved all the way, although watch out for the occasional deep pothole. The views are excellent, cloud and haze permitting. The scenery changes from pine to mixed forest and back again intermingled with coffee on the steep hillsides. There are regular small settlements all the way, Chinacla, is being promoted as a Lenca community to visit, and is a pleasant place to stop, without there being much to do.

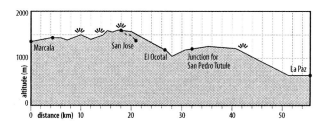

San Jose is large village 25km from Marcala, and a few km downhill from Pedina on the highway, ask for Nayo and Vinda who are well known locally and can organise accommodation and visits to nearby Lenca communities.

There are several more valleys to cross, some deep, on the way to the junction for San Pedro Tutule. It's another 28km to La Paz, and after a gentle climb the road is almost entirely downhill, although there are a couple of short climbs out of valleys nearer the base of the mountains. Occasional comedors provide food break possibilites. The pine forest gradually thins with descent and there are good views all the way down to the to the plains from where there are gentler gradients through an arid landscape to La Paz.

La Paz
There is not much in this town for tourists, although it's pleasant enough and a convenient place to stop off for the night on the way to or back from the mountains. A weekly market on Saturdays brings a little life. Onwards are two roads; one unpaved that goes direct to Comayagua, or a paved wide road, that crosses the plain, turn left at the junction with the main intercity route.

There are 2 buses up to Goajiquiro at midday and half an hour afterwards.

La Paz/Comayagua to Tegucigalpa(☞ see p.124), 70km – This intercity highway can be very busy, but there is space on the roadside for cycling. There's a long climb out of the Humuya river basin, the heavy traffic tends to bunch together emitting clouds of unpleasant fumes, although there are excellent views behind, of the valley below. The scenery is mostly pine forest, with a few isolated settlements. The road then drops, with good views onto a bleak high plain, before descending toward the capital. Taking one of the many buses, avoids the traffic.

Comayagua

This colonial town has a couple of impressive churches, and other nice architecture and some lively markets. Banking and internet facilities are available along with a good range of accommodation and places to eat. The tourist office is on the north side of the main plaza, they can help with current information and basic maps as facilities in the nearby national park are gradually being developed.

Montanas de Comayagua National Park
The mountains rising above Comayagua are incredibly beautiful, and relatively easy to reach via old logging roads.

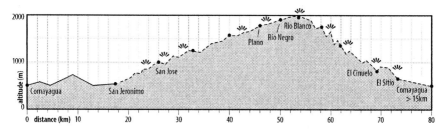

Rio Negro is the only place offering accommodation, even then its only lodging with a local guide, although camping is possible on the football pitch as well. Unmarked trails climb up into the forest and to local waterfalls. A visitors centre is planned for the future.

There are two roads to get there from Comayagua, the easiest option goes north via a paved road to San Jeronimo, which has a hospedaje and a couple of comedors. Branch right into the village, and then turn right after 200m (ask directions for San Jose if unsure), this road passes a football pitch on the left and climbs into the pine forest. There are two or three small rivers to ford and short, steep climbs afterwards, before reaching the village of San Jose(shop). Turn right, there are only a couple of steeper sections, and a few streams to ford. For the most part it's well graded, and climbs through the edge of the forest passing a few villages with shops, the occcasional views are exceptional, Rio Negro is another 23km.

There is a beautiful circular route back to Comayagua, shown in the above X section, although this track can be extremely hardwork(ask locally for advice). Continue climbing around the mountainside from Rio Negro to Rio Blanco, from where it's predominately downhill. The track continues through countless beautiful side valleys where there are streams to ford. There are several smaller tracks heading left, up into the mountains. Keep checking with locals on which is the right route and eventually reach the lovely village of El Cinuelo(shops).

109

Onwards the dirt road is in much better condition, there's one last climb into pine woodland, before descending to El Sitio and down the gentle gradients to Comayagua. *NB This route would be very difficult after prolonged rain, the tracks are very steep in places so don't underestimate the time needed for this journey.*

Central Honduras

Comayagua to lago Yojoa, about 60km – This route has only been cycled from Siguetepeque, from where there is a gentle climb up to a stunning descent to Taulabe. From Comayagua there is a significant climb out of the Humuya valley toward Siguetepeque. The road has enough space for cycling although there are occasional significant differences in the level of the road, where re-surfacing work has taken place.

☞ see p.105 for route description from **Siguetepeque to Lago Yojoa**.

Comayagua–Minas de Oro and onto Yoro

There are several interesting variations to this trip, both go through San Jeronimo. The main bus route continues on the paved road to San Antonio before turning right and climbing up the dirt road to Los Puentes and Las Crucitas. The alternative is climbing up to San Jose from San Jeronimo and turning left toward La Laguna, and Tres Pinos, rejoining the main road at Los Puentes. This is not an easy route with panniers, but the dirt roads are very quiet, in reasonable condition and the scenery stunning.

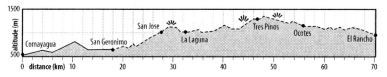

From San Jose the road climbs steadily through the woods and coffee farms with a couple of steeper granny gear sections. It then drops down to a pretty lake, where there is one basic shop. The next village is Las Crucitas, the tracks have partial shading and are often lined with flowers. There are a couple of climbs, a steep descent, and a stream to cross on the way, the last km and a half being particularly hard work, however the incredible views from **Tres Pinos** make the climbing worthwhile.

There are a couple of shops and opportunities from this village to walk up to the national park; a track climbs, steeply in places through small coffee plantations, to the edge of the forest, from where there are footpaths, with superb views. For exploring the park interior, employing a guide is recommended.

From Tres Pinos there's another short climb then a longer descent to the junction at Los Puentes (shop), the village itself is a bit further downhill. Turning right the road descends and climbs a small valley before entering Las Crucitas, this is not a place to spend much time, although there are shops for supplies. The next section through the pine forest is beautiful and very peaceful, although there are a several hills and occasional lumbering cattle on the road.

Rancho Grande is a very spread out settlement, with a mixture of wooden houses, and a few older buildings, there are several comedors and shops and a basic hospedaje opposite the church on the far side of the river. Whilst pleasant enough, if possible aim to get to Esquias for the night which is a lovely small town.

This involves a climb into the pine forest, the road then divides turn right for the direct

route to Esquias, left goes via San Luis. This road seems to double back on itself along a ridge, and offers good views back over the Comayagua mountains. After a few km there's a long undulating descent passing through small settlements into the Esquias valley. A couple of rivers are crossed, with ranches inbetween, before a short climb into town.

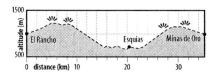

Esquias is a delightful town in the middle of nowhere, there are 2 hospedajes and a couple of places to eat by the tree lined square.

From **Esquias** there are two routes to **Minas de Oro**:

1) The old route (La ruta viejo) – It goes from the back of town, it's worth checking which way, as it isn't obvious. It climbs up a small track into the pine forest, and is wonderfully peaceful, with good shade. It's difficult to get lost as the main route is clear. There may be some cattle grazing or a wood cutter, but there are no houses, and a pleasant sense of remoteness. The track is generally in good condion and the gradients mostly gentle, but at the beginning and end of the climb there are steeper, stonier sections. From the pass there are good views (especially at sunset) and a junction:

Right – descends a rough stoney track to Minas de Oro;

Left – leads into the mountains and could be worth exploring with time to spare.

2) The new route – It is almost a third longer and has added perils of dust as the occasional bus or truck passes. There are a couple of shops and a comedor at the junction with the road toward El Porvenir. The road then climbs, it can be hard work with the lack of shade, but is rewarded with good views higher up, before descending into the valley of Minas de Oro.

Minas de Oro

This gorgeous colonial town is set in a valley basin, surrounded by pine forested mountains. The cobbled streets and stone buildings are mostly in good condition, with a couple of interesting decaying ruins. As it's name suggests, Minas de Oro was once very wealthy, now it's a sleepy place, and a great place to relax. There are a couple of basic hospedajes and a few places to eat.

SIDE TRIPS
The tracks into the hills to the west of town look interesting, although are unresearched. The descent to Victoria is worth doing even if not planning to head further in this direction, there's a bus back to Minas de Oro mid-afternoon.

Minas de Oro to Yoro or Sulaco – There are two ways out of town:
The old semi-cobbled street, goes from the north west corner of the plaza, crosses a stream and climbs past the chapel on the hill. The other better quality dirt road, is a continuation of the road from Esquias, both routes meet a couple of km further uphill.

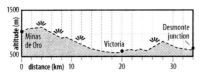

The road gently climbs through pretty countryside, dotted with rock outcrops, to a pass, with beautiful long distance views over to the Montanas de la Flor. Descending through the trees, the first junction right leads down to San Jose Portrero, where apparently there is a hospedaje, but check first.

The dirt road continues downhill through a few small settlements and over a couple of rivers with short climbs afterwards. Lower down, on the plains, there's a bridge over the wide Sulaco river, which offers a cooling swim. Shortly after comes the village of Victoria, the road straight on continues to Santa Cruz de Yojoba, but is unresearched. Take the turning right that climbs up into this village, which has a nice hospedaje and a couple of comedors. Onwards the dirt road becomes a little more stoney, but is still a very pleasant ride, climbing through patches of forest and higher up, scrub and small farms. Whilst climbing up to the pass, there are excellent views looking back over the plains and river, especially approaching sunset. Just over the other side is the village of Las Canas with a couple of basic shops. Keep descending into the plains, the road comes to a junction after a few more km.

Onward options:
1) **To Sualaco 6km, and onto the Montanas de la Flor:**
Turn right and continue through the dry plains, it's a gentle downhill with a couple dips for bridges. Sulaco has a couple of places to stay and eat. There's not a great deal to do, but the river is close by and the town friendly enough to spend the night.

Further south over the foot hills is the town of Marale, a bit run down, but pleasant, with a basic hospedaje and a couple of comedors. There is a route from 4km further south on the road to Porvenir into the Montana de la Flor anthropological reserve. It is beautiful, but the climbing is steep. It passes through several different types of forest and offers excellent views. There are indigenous communities in the hills, but little or no information on how to visit them. This route was explored as far as the community of El Cacao(shop), onwards the dirt road seems in good condition and could be an interesting route to Campamento on the Juticalpa road.

2) To Yoro, about 45km:
Turn left, the road starts to climb into the hills. Its 4km to the village of San Antonio where there are some warmish springs and beautiful river rapids with a natural bridge, 3km from the road. Turn right and descend into the village, it's possible to cycle to the river, then walk, or take the footpath from the village. Ask for directions to the puente natural.

Continuing through the hills, there are some large trees lining the road side. The route is pretty, and there are a couple of small settlements on the way for basic food and drink.

This main road is currently being improved, and in the next few years will be part of a paved route from Yoro to Talanga.

Yoro
This is a modern provincial town, with large markets catering for a wide rural area. There are a few places to stay, many restaurants and cafes. A couple of places provide internet, although it's very hard to get up-to-date tourist information, the disused office in the middle of the plaza used to provide it.

There are routes into the Montanas de la Flor national park from Yoro, and with reasonable Spanish, try the municipal offices for up to date national park information. One suggestion was to walk or cycle southwest to the aldea of San Jose, where it's possible to camp, apparently there are guides available for onwards exploration to pretty places like the Lagunas de Ojos Negros.

Yoro to Santa Rita (for onward routes to Lago Yojoa, Tela or San Pedro Sula) – The road is gradually being improved, with new bridges and regrading.

The ride from Yoro through the plains is straightforward, but not particularly interesting, and there is no shade. The long descent into a deep valley has good views, although the temperatures rise rapidly. The valley gradually widens into hot plains around El Negrito 30km from Yoro, although narrows again, before a climb over hills, and then dropping down into Santa Rita.

☞ see p.117 for routes to **Tela**

For San Pedro, there is an unresearched short cut to the main intercity highway, on the west side of the plains.

For Lago Yojoa turn right and continue to the junction called La Barca. Turn left for the quickest route on the highway to La Guama, near the lake. Turning right for a couple of km, then left, is longer, but is a quieter route up to Pena Blanca, and the Pulhapanzak waterfalls.

Lago Yojoa

The lake on it's own would be worth a visit, and there are some interesting off-road side trips into the two mountain ranges nearby. At lake level, there is more mixed forest to the south, pines dominate the northern side. It's an area famed for good bird watching, and the north shore has hotels where 400 species of birds have been seen. On the south side of the lake, 3km along the road toward Santa Barbara, are several fish restaurants, they offer good food, excellent views, especially at sunset, and basic accommodation if required.

Pena Blanca near the north shore is a good base for exploring the Santa Barbara National Park, there are a few places to stay. A nearby bridge over the river from the lake is a popular place to swim. There are interesting pre-Colombian ruins a few km away on the lake shore at Los Naranjos. The junction is just east of Pena Blanca and, then 4-5km on a dirt road to the lake shore, it's worth doing for the lake views even if the ruins don't hold enough interest. The Pulhanpanzak waterfalls have been recommended by several people and are 10km north of town, near the village of San Buenaventura, they do get busy at weekends.

114

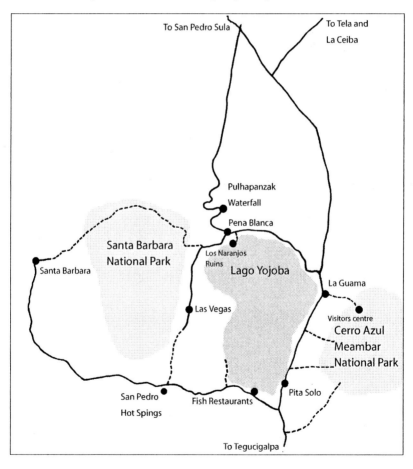

Also from Pena Blanca are tough, but beautiful rides over the mountains to hot springs at San Pedro via Las Vegas, and up to and beyond Los Laureles at the edge the National Park.

There are a few more expensive accommodation options, near excellent bird watching, along various points of the north shore, between Pena Blanca and La Guama.

☞ see p.117 for **Lago Yojoa** to **Tela**

Lago Yojoa to Santa Barbara, 55km – A very quiet, good quality road. There are a couple of small hills, the largest nearer the lake. If there is no cloud, there are excellent views of the Santa Barbara national park, otherwise a few small settlements in mixed farmland, and pine forest on the higher ground. There are thermal sprints at San Pedro, a couple of km south of the road. At the same junction, a dirt road cuts north over the edge of the park to Las Vegas and eventually Pena Blancas.

Santa Barbara

This town has become wealthy from the coffee plantations in the hills to the south. It's a pleasant place to relax, being off the main tourist trail. From the square are views of the National park There is a road up from behind the town that climbs up to a local landmark fort. It's easier to get access to the National Park from the Lago Yojoa side, although there is an unexplored mule track through to Pena Blanca, it's a big climb from this side.

The coffee growing areas further west are also interesting. The road from San Nicholas toward Atima goes up a pretty valley if wanting to explore and the former has a lot of character.

The Santa Barbara National Park and beyond

To get there, take the paved road to Las Vegas, it continues level for a few km, before starting to climb steeply through a village. The track around the edge of the national park starts from a turning right near the top of this village, it isn't obvious, ask if unsure. The paved road continues to Las Vegas, from where there are unexplored rough roads through to the hot springs at San Pedro on the Santa Barbara road.

The track to Los Laureles continues to climb steeply, the views of the cloud forest higher up and later on, the lake, are beautiful. This steep track has been partially researched, it's unexplored all the way to Santa Barbara, and locals say that parts of it are only good enough for mules, still it could be an adventure! There are local guides (apparently needed) available for climbing the peak.

The Cerro Azul Meambar National Park

There is access into this park at several points along the eastern side of the lake, from Jardines to La Guama. From the later is a 7km route to the visitors centre. It's a steady climb on dirt roads, there are waterfalls, wildlife and good rough tracks for exploration.

Lago Yojoa to San Pedro Sula, 65km – The easiest, quietest route is from Pena Blanca. The road descends steadily, twisting and turning through the lush vegetation and patches of woodland. Eventually reaching the agricultural plains of sugar cane, the road continues for 10km before reaching the main road. Onwards the road is busy, although there is plenty of space for cycling.

There are buses direct to San Pedro, but with time, it's worth cycling the section down to the intercity road, there are plenty of buses passing this junction.

The Caribbean coast and islands

San Pedro Sula

This lively city competes for attention with the capital, although it doesn't have half the character. It does have all the normal attractions, if wanting to catch a film etc. The markets are busy and interesting, and spread over several streets, there are distinct sections for vegetable, fruits and hardware.

There are direct buses if required to Tela, La Ceiba, Yoro (including Minas de Oro), Copan ruinas, Sant Rosa de Copan, Neuvo Octepeque (including the frontier Agua Caliente), La Esperanza, and all destinations on the route to Tegucigalpa.

San Pedro Sula to Puerto Cortes and Omoa, 72km – It's a 4-lane road to Pto Cortes, and can be very hot and the road busy, but the ride is safe with plenty of space for cycling on the side of the road. With limited time it might be better to bus to Puerto Cortes, and cycle the last 20km from there.

The views on the way overlook the agricultural plains, and up into the forested hills, there are many places to stop for a break. From Puerto Cortes, the route follows the coast, although there are not many views of the sea. This road is quieter and is gradually being upgraded – it should soon be completely paved to meet up with the new road from Puerto Barrios.

Regular minibuses, with roof racks, service the route to Puerto Cortes.

Omoa

This growing Caribbean village is a nice place for a stop-off, it's a very popular resort for the city folk of San Pedro, along with many backpackers and a few Guatemalans. From the main road it's another 2km to the beaches. On the way there's a large castle, and a few bars and shops. Accommodations, from hostels and hammocks to hotels are along or close to the beach front.

Inland there are waterfalls and river pools to swim in, if wanting a bit of solitude. Follow the track on the other side of the main road into the foothills, there are many paths, and further up it becomes difficult to cycle.

Omoa to Pto Barrios, Guatemala about 85km – A nice ride, the dirt road is at present being upgraded to meet with the paved Guatemalan road at El Corinto. The road is quiet, but this will gradually change when it's paved all the way. The scenery is lush and green, with good views up into the mountains and for the first few km, out to sea. There are a few small settlements, many ranches, and numerous rivers to cross. The road is not completely flat, but the only hilly section is just before the border, and has a bit more shade.

The Honduran migration office is small, but easy to see as the money changers hang around outside. Formalities are simple, there may be a small exit tax.

From the Honduran border, the road crosses the hot Motugua plains, there's little shade and banana plantations as far as the eye can see. A couple of worker settlements, have basic comedors if needed. The Guatemalan border post is a few km after crossing the Rio Motugua. Entre Rios, another 10km or so has a few places to eat.

NB There are regular aerial crop sprayings, by some reports they can be indiscriminate.

The highway on to Puerto Barrios is busy with heavy traffic, however it is mainly downhill, and there is some space at the side of the road to cycle.

☞ see p.91 for **Puerto Barrios**

Lago Yojoa-La Ceiba

Lago Yojoa (Pena blanca) to Progresso 70km – It's prettier and quieter descending from the Pena blanca side of the lake, there's lush scenery and passes by the Pulhanpanzak waterfalls. Lower down, as the road levels out, there are large sugar cane plantations, ranches and increased temperatures. At the junction with the interctiy main road, turn right for a few km to the next main junction (La Barca), and turn left. This road is not busy, and crosses the plain and a couple of rivers to Santa Rita, before undulating along the side of the hills to **Progresso.** This is a large, busy and modern town, there's little to interest tourists, but a mix of accommodation if needing to overnight. It's a good place stock up on bike spares.

Progresso to Tela, 61km – A hot route, lots of water will be needed. The highway gradually descends off the agricultural plains around Progresso, and is in places very pretty as it crosses a few hills, where there are a few small rivers, with pools to bathe in if needing too cool down.

After 40km or so the road starts to descend steadily into the coconut palm plantations on the coast, and this is the rather monotonous scenery for quite a few km. It seems to take along time to reach Tela, the advertising starts several km before the town, which is a couple of km downhill from a busy junction on the highway.

Tela

This town is a good mix of garifuna and latin cultures. There are nice local beaches, although on the down side crime has in the past been a problem. The lively weekend nightlife is renowned, this can be a good place to meet fellow travellers. Accommodations in the town are mostly on the beach, catering for all budgets.

West of town, the ride along the coastal dirt road to Tornabe and Miami, passes through a couple of run down settlements, then the scenery is all white sand and palm trees. **Tornabe** is a beautiful, small village and has a couple of places to stay, or camping is possible on the beach. There are a few sea food restaurants, the beaches are beautiful and it's very relaxed.

The sandy track continues on to the smaller and even more peaceful settlement of Miami, although may be difficult on bike.

SIDE TRIPS
Punta Sal National park
There are various agencies in town specialising in tours. It is an excellent trip, there are reefs to snorkle, pristine beaches, monkeys, and trails to walk. The boat ride across the bay can be bruising if the wind is up.

Alternatively it should be possible to walk from the village of Miami along the beach.

Tela to La Ceiba, 100km – The good quality road makes for a pleasant ride, there is a gradual climb up over a small ridge near the km176 marker, otherwise it's gentle undulation or flat. There are regular settlements with shops and comedors. Nearer La Ceiba are excellent views of the imposing Pico Bonita national park, although the mountain tops are often covered in cloud. The side trip to the Cuero y Salado wildlife reserve (see below) is worth considering, although some return disappointed with the lack of visible wildlife.

Cuero y Salado wildlife reserve
This reserve of mangrove wetlands is home to the reclusive Manatee, with boat access to nature rich waterways.

To get there, turn off the highway onto dusty roads at La Union, about 35km from La Ceiba. For the last 8km, requires either paying for transport along the local railway or a bumpy ride

117

along and/or beside the tracks, which start at the east end of La Union. Take some food, as supplies at the village in the reserve are limited. It is possible to stay at the wardens residence, either camping or renting a room. There is plenty of fish for sale and coconuts in abundance.

To explore the reserve there are canoes for hire and the warden does guided tours by motorboat, if there's a tour coming through, it may be possible to tack on the end of it.

La Ceiba

This lively comercial city is easy to explore on bike, and has an amazing back drop of the Pico Bonita mountains. There is the usual mix of accommodation, with the cheaper options near the old railway line to the docks and on the eastern side of town with all the nightlife, just back from the beach. There are some good street food stalls and markets spread around the central area.
☞ see p.119 for onward routes

SIDE TRIP
The ride up the Cangrejel valley by the Pico Bonita national park is stunning ☞ see p.120

The Bay Islands

The ferries for the Bay islands go from docks a few km east of La Ceiba.
Cross the bridge on the main road toward Saba and after a couple of km turn left, it's another 3km to the docks. Check the departure times in La Ceiba, as there is only one boat a day to Utila and one to Roatan. The docks are modern, with one or two comedors, but no shops.

The ferry company does try to charge significantly for bicycles, although the weight would normally be under their baggage limits. Haggling can work, and on the way back taking a bike for free doesn't seem so much of a problem.
NB There are no scheduled boats between Utila and Roatan.

Utila is an island almost completely dedicated to diving, although the snorkling can be good as well. There are bicycles everywhere, and they a good way to get about.
On **Guanaja** a bicycle would be a pain as almost all the transport is by motor launch.

Roatan

This beautiful island offers the best options for cycling. The roads are nearly all paved, with a few dusty tracks through the forest in the north/east. There is a backbone of hills, which vary in height, and give excellent views where the road crosses them. It has been well developed for tourism and there are several resorts, although it's still possible to leave the hoards behind.

The most pleasant way to cycle to the western end of the island, is to head south west from the port,**Coxen hole,** along the sandy coastal road, and turn right after a few km at the junction with a paved road. This climbs for a couple of km into the forested hills with some good views. At the summit, there's a junction; left leads down to **West Bay**, which has a wonderful beach with restaurants, hotels and some excellent snorkelling. Right goes down to **West End**, which is the most popular backpacker base, with wonderful beaches, snorkling and diving, as well as being a fun place to relax.

The paved road between Coxen hole and West End is relatively uninteresting, although it passes a quiet village, Sandy bay, which has access to beaches, and a couple of places to stay. Northeast of Coxen Hole the road climbs over a couple of small hills, passing Brick bay (with several marinas) and a few other resorts.
French Bay is a working port town and appears more wealthy than Coxen hole, it has a yachting club which is a good place for making contact if looking for work on boats, and has a couple of places to stay.

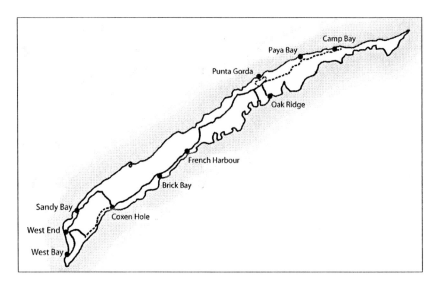

Continuing, the road starts to climb through small villages and lush vegetation over the islands backbone, with amazing views eastwards at the high point. It then drops down to the junctions for Punta Gorda and Oak Ridge. Both communities have the charm of being a bit run down, but the people are friendly and give a good insight into the islands culture.
Oak Ridge is spread around a small surrounded by mangroves, there are a few hotels, restaurants and launches out to the caye.
Punta Gorda is spread along the beach of the northern coast, there is access at both ends, so a round route is possible. For a chance to try the local garifuna food, this is the best place. Further on the roads get very dusty, although there are few cars, take some supplies as there are few shops. It's worth cycling as far as **Camp Bay** at the eastern end of the island. This is a wonderfully peaceful community as yet untouched by resort development, with some deserted beaches nearby. The Paya resort has a nice beaches and there are other turnings to resorts on the southern coast

Beyond Camp bay is a track, after climbing for a couple of km the route has been gated by the property owner. It's possible to walk further, through gaps in the fence for another couple of km for superb views over the eastern end of island.

Onwards routes from La Ceiba
There are two basic choices:
1) Inland, south over the mountains via Olanchito and La Union (La Muralla National Park)
There are two ways to Olanchito:
A beautiful route through the mountains via the Cangrejel valley and Yaruca (☞ see p.120) Or on the busy paved coastal road via La Saba. For the second option it's worth considering taking a bus, as this route is not particularly interesting.

From Olanchito to La Union would be a long days ride, there is only one settlement of any size on this 90km road, and some significant climbing. The junction for this route is 13km east of Olanchito, 42km west of Saba.
The first part of this route is incorrectly marked on the ITMB map
☞ see p.128 for this route described in reverse.

2) Toward Trujillo, with a route South via Oriente Bonita and San Esteban to Catacamas/Juticalpa.
The route along the main highway to Sava can be busy, although the road is in good condition and there good views through the lush vegetation.
The route marked on the ITMB map from Jutiapa to Trujillo along the coast, only goes as far as Rio Coco (about 30km), in good condition, from where people use a weekly boat service. (☞ see p.122 for route description in reverse) This may change in the future, check locally for up to date information
From Sava the scenery is mainly agricultural, with monotonous coconut plantations lining the road nearer Trujillo.

La Ceiba to Yaruca (up the Cangrejel valley), 21km – This route travels up one of the most beautiful valleys in Central America. There are good views up into the forest and mountains all

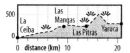

the way up to Yaruca. A new walkway is planned for crossing the river with trails into the park on the other side, however it's been talked about for a long time. There has also been talk of flooding this valley, by building a dam for hydro-electricity.
The route starts on the eastside of the new Saipan bridge, on the road toward Saba. Although the junction may be unclear (ask for the road to Yaruca), the route follows the river all the way up the valley. The dirt road is in reasonable condition, although after heavy rain may be difficult. There are a couple of places for food near Las Pitres, and occcasional shops as well, the river is excellent for swimming, having numerous pools in between the large rocks.
NB There is an outdoor pursuits centre (Omega tours) just before the village of Las Mangas, where numerous activities are available, as well as lodging and camping. The hosts are very knowledgable of the local area.
The gradients are easy up until the river crossing at las Naranjas, the following 3km has a steep climb up the side of the valley, the excellent views from the top of the pass make it worthwhile. The road then drops down into the Yaruca basin, it's mainly ranch land, but again there are stunning views of the surrounding mountains from a different perspective. Yaruca itself is a sleepy large village, and has little to detain anyone.
Onwards, the road climbs gently up a river valley through a couple more settlements, before a short steep hairpin up to the end of road.

Yaruca to Olanchito, about 50km
NB Reasonable off-roading skills are required. The full route with panniers is tough as it involves short sections of walking and carrying the bike over some streams. The climb will involve about 20% walking. It would be easier by leaving bags behind and doing a circular route by taking a bus back to La Ceiba from Olanchito, and should be possible in a day, if starting early.
The ITMB map shows this old route through to Olanchito, these days it's little more than a footpath in places.

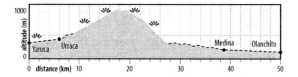

It will take several hours to get to Olanchito and crossing the pass there is no where to buy food, and only one or two isolated houses. Although there are a couple of springs nearer the top of the pass if needed.

From the end of the road above Urraca, the track/footpath climbs steadily, there is bad erosion in a couple of places, but it's possible to cycle as the gradients are good. There are several small streams, and fallen trees to cross, it will be necessary to carry bikes for a few metres over these obstacles. The route then gradually bends around to the left, climbing all the time, in and out of 3 headlands, before heading toward a gap in the mountains. The views at the pass, both north and south are superb, and there a couple of nice trees to sit under for shade. There may be the sounds of the occasional farmer clearing land on the slopes below.

Once over the pass the track starts to descend, steeply in places. There is one small climb after passing through a gate, then it's all downhill, occasionally very steep. It's worth stopping occasionally to take in the view, as most of the time will be spent concentrating on not falling off. As it starts to level off, there's another gate, with a track off to the right, keep following the river on the left side, this track fords it later on. It then gets wider and passes through a few small settlements, as it undulates toward Medina at the junction on the Olanchito road, and the first place with shops. Onwards, this main road is dusty, wide and mostly flat, for the last 10km to Olanchito.

Olanchito
This town sits in the middle of dusty plains and is surprisingly prosperous. There are good markets, banks, internet facilities, and a couple of pensions and hospedajes. It's not a place to head for, but pleasant enough for a night if passing through.

The bus station, has services to Yoro, La Union for La Muralla NP, Trujillo, Saba and La Ceiba.
Olanchito to Yoro – This route hasn't been researched because the road is notoriously dusty, with road improvements it might be worth considering, as it passes through some pretty hill country.

Olanchito to Trujillo, 140km – This road is fast and the gradients are all gentle, although the scenery can be monotonous and is predominately agricultural, with many coconut plantations nearer Trujillo. If the cloud is high there will good views of the mountains to the south. Buses pass through Saba and Tocoa which are the main commercial towns for this part of the coast, and transport hubs, although have little of interest for the average tourist. The road is not the most interesting, there isn't much shade and it can be very hot, so taking a bus is a reasonable choice.

121

Trujillo
This historic town has a certain run-down charm. There are several cafes, bars and places to eat, although the beaches are the best reason for coming. It's a good place to relax and there are a variety of places to stay in the town and nearby.

SIDE TRIPS
The mountains behind the town are unresearched, but are reputed to have beautiful views, the bay islands are visible on a clear day. There is a 4 wheel drive track to the summit, which should be cycleable.

Ask at the port for the times of boats, if interested in travelling toward La Mosquita, or west toward Guadaloupe and Rio Coco, occassionally there are boats to the Bay islands as well.

An untried, recommended cycling route was from Trujillo via Bonita Orriental eastwards, through the numerous Garifuna settlements along the coast.

Trujillo to La Ceiba (along the coast), about 80km – This route is a bit of an adventure, but does require a bit of forethought. Following the coast along from Trujillo, is a relatively easy dirt road, there are numerous streams to ford, all possible on a bike in the dry season. The beaches are gorgeous, and there's good fish in the local eateries.

It's about 10km to **Santa Fe**, and possible to stay either in a hostel or camping on the beach, but security has been an issue in the area. The next small town is San Antonio after a few km, and a few minutes after, Guadaloupe. This is by far the nicest fishing settlement along this stretch of coast and the last reachable village on the existing road.

The ITMB map shows a track carrying on, this does exist, but apparently is very hard work, it maybe worth asking if it has been improved, as it would no doubt be a stunning route to ride

Onwards, the easiest option is to hitch a ride on the express launch, which makes the trip along the coast once or twice a week. Ask locally in Trujillo when it's running. To get onboard, it's necessary to stand on the beach and wave like hell as it's passing until the boat comes ashore. It would be easier to board in Trujillo, but this might mean missing the ride along the coast. Settlements passed in order from Guadaloupe are:

Puerto Batilda, Plan Grande, Quinito, Manatee, Puerto Escondid, Rio Coco

The price of of the boat isn't fixed and it's necessary to have passage as far as Rio Coco in order to strike rideable road again. The coastline is idyllic, and the boat may take some time, dropping people off with their supplies.

From Rio Coco, a 26km dirt road winds in and out of coastal settlements all the way to Jutiapa on the main road to La Ceiba. There are several fordings, some quite deep, although they will gradually be bridged. It's another 35km along the main road to La Ceiba.

Trujillo–Catacamas/Juticalpa

Parts of this route are beautiful, although there are some longish, flat monotonous sections, which may be worth taking alternative transport through:
FromTrujillo to the beginning of the hills near La Esperanza, the ranchland plains around San Esteban and the paved road between Juticalpa to Catacamas.
NB. Speeding cowboy pick-up drivers and the dust they create, can be an occasional worry on this route.

Trujillo to San Esteban, 119km – The road is paved as far as Bonita Orriental, afterwards it becomes a wide dusty road, with small settlements stretched along it's sides.

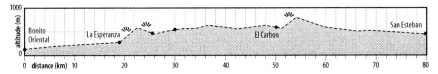

The first significant climb into the hills brings much improved views, with larger patches of forest and more interesting scenery. The gradients are not too steep and the dust from passing vehicles is the only major problem. From El Carbon, the road climbs a few hundred metres through some forested foothills, and then drops into the Rio Grande basin, on this section there are not many places for provisions until hitting town.

San Esteban itself is not a very exciting place to head for, just a functional agricultural settlement, with basic accommodations and comedors. It would be more pleasant to explore camping possibilities in the hills in or around El Carbon.

San Esteban to Gualaco, 42km – The first part of this route is across hot and flat plains, with ranch land on either side disappearing off into the distance. The road is dusty, so starting early to avoid the pickups and lack of shade is advisable. There may be good views of the Sierra de Agalta, but the mountains are often covered in a haze.

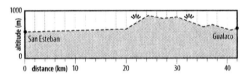

After 25km the road starts to climb into sparsely pine forested slopes, and winds around the hills before descending toward Gualaco. There is little shade on any of this route, although there are occasional agricultural settlements on the plains, with a small shop or two.

Gualaco

This small town is trying to become a base for exploring the Sierra Agalta NP. There is an information centre on the western edge of town, from where guides can be organised for trekking to the local peaks. There are a couple of comedors and a few shops.

The nearby caves are worth a visit, head towards Jicalapa and ask directions locally as the tracks can be confusing. It's possible to swim into the lower caves, a waterproof head torch and snorkel makes it more fun. A guide might be helpful, as it can be unnerving exploring these caves alone.

Gualaco to Juticalpa, 55km or Catacamas, 90km – The first part of this route is through mountains and beautiful pine woodland scenery with some great views, although not without some hard climbing and the road is in poor condition in places.

From Gualaco the dirt road descends to a bridge after a couple of km, and then starts climbing into the mountains. There are several false summits and dips making it tiring, the road passes a couple of small settlements but there are few opportunities for refilling water bottles or to buy food. The pass has excellent views westwards, a great place to see the sunset, it's then a long, well graded downhill all the way to San Francisco de la Paz, which can be quite a buzz. This is a quiet settlement to spend the night if needed, there are two basic accommodation options near the main square.

123

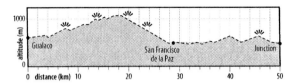

Onwards, the scenery is much drier there is a lot of undulation, with a couple of longer climbs. There are only ranchitos on this road and no opportunities to buy food until the junction with the main road at Telica.

This highway is paved, flat and quite fast, there are good views westwards heading in either direction. It's worth taking the diversion to Catacamas for the caves of Talagua and the surrounding steep valleys and forest, there are regular buses if time is short.

Catacamas

This spreadout town on the lower slopes of the Sierra Agalta has a relaxed and pleasant atmosphere. There are large markets, cafes, banking facilities and a variety of accommodation.

The nearby **Caves of Talagua** and the surrounding mountains are the main reason for coming to the town. The 10km ride to the caves takes less than an hour. The road heads north from the top of town near the markets. It's a pleasant ride on dirt roads through farmland and small villages, before climbing gently up a pretty river valley into the national park.
NB Take a torch, or preferably a headlamp.

The caves are extensive and have an interesting history attached to them, a guide will show you around in small groups . There's also a museum and restaurant on the site. Further up this beautiful valley, the forest screams with life. There are short walks to other caves up river, take plenty of water as there is none en route.

Ask the wardens about guided tours to the peaks of the Sierra Agalta, it takes less time to walk from Catacamas than from Gualaco.

Juticalpa

This modern busy town doesn't have a lot for tourists, but is nice enough, if needing to overnight. The centre is a couple of km west of the highway, there several accommodation options a block or so from the main square.

There are buses to La Union for La Muralla national park and a variety of services to the Capital, the bus station is close to the highway.

Juticalpa/Catacamas toward Tegucigalpa

This main road can have some fast traffic in places, there are occasionally good distant views, but the surrounding scenery is uninteresting and unless with a lot of time it's worth taking the bus.
From **Limones**, ☞ see p.127 for the route north to **La Union and the Caribbean**.
From **Guimaca**, ☞ see p.126 for the route heading south toward the Danli road.
From **Talanga**, ☞ see p.125 for the route to the El Tigre national park, which cuts through to the capital via the pretty Valle de Angeles and Santa Lucia.

Tegucigalpa
There is an plan of the city on the ITMB map
There are two main parts to this city divided by the muddy Choluteca river. Tegucigalpa is to the north, and has the more developed shopping and recreational facilities, as well as the cathedral, nearby which the cheap accommodation can be found. More expensive options are further east, near the embassies and consulates.

On the other side of the river is Comayaguela, where the markets are lively, but there is little else for travellers, apart from the variety of terminals for buses to various parts of the country. The airport is 7km south of the city on the busy expressway.
El Tigre National Park – It's not every Capital that has cloud forest on it's doorstep. Cycling up to the wealthy suburb of El Hatillo is no small climb, and at weekends the local enthusiasts will be out in their racing gear, there are good views over the city below. The road continues through woodland and small settlements (with basic shops) to the park entrance.
A route is shown on the ITMB map as going all the way through to El Rosario, but in places it's only a footpath.

The wardens may not be too happy about people cycling through the park to San Juancita, but you can only ask!

To Comayagua or La Paz – This route is one of the busiest in the country, however the road does have space for cycling, and there are some lovely forested sections before the road drops into Humuya valley. Overall it's worth taking a bus if time is of the essence.
☞ see p.128 for the route to **Yuscaran**, **Danli** and **Nicaragua**

South to the Pacific coast was left unresearched due to the incredible heat, although the Isla de Tigra in the Golfo de Fonesca, has a road around it and could be fun.

Tegucigalpa–El Tigre national park–Talanga

There's a long 10km climb up to the colonial mining town of **Santa Lucia**, although the road is well graded. It's well geared up for tourism with it's good views and classic architecture being the selling points. The Peace corps training centre for Honduras is based nearby, and may be a useful place to ask for information if wishing to explore remote areas.

Onwards there's not too much more climbing, as the road winds around the edge of the national park, giving occasional good views through the shady pine forest.

Valle de Angeles is 28km from the Capital and is an attractive town, it specialises in wooden handicrafts, but sells artisania in many shops from all over Honduras. Accommodation and food are predictably more expensive, as this is a tour destination.

It's another 16km to **San Juancita,** there's a short, but steep climb out of Valle de Angeles, the road then follows the contours for a few km with gradual descent to the peaceful village, where there's a couple of comedors and basic accommodation. It's a very steep 5km climb (may be better to walk) up to the El Tigre national park, on a dirt track. The visitors centre is at El Rosario, an old mining settlement.

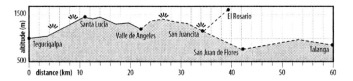

El Tigre National Park

There are several different trails within the park, a map is given on paying the entrance fee. Walks of a variety of lengths are well marked, with occasional good lookouts, as ever wildlife is best seen and heard in the very early mornings and at dusk.

Apparently there's a cabin to rent by the visitors centre, most have said booking isn't necessary, although it would be worth avoiding the national holidays and weekends. It's something you may feel you deserve after the climb and it also gives the chance to see and hear the wildlife in the early morning. Camping should be possible, if the above option is full, or stay in San Juancita.

San Juancita to Talanga, 30km (or back to Danli highway) – From San Juancita, the dusty road drops away quickly into drier vegetation with increased temperatures. Bear left at the edge of the small settlement of San Juan de Flores, and after crossing the river the road starts climbing gently, once over the small ridge, there's a gradual descent through farmland into Talanga. This is a pleasant town, with some accommodation if needed.

Turning right at San Juan de Flores leads back to the Danli road and is unresearched, but looks a reasonable dirt road, it would make a useful cut through if heading toward Nicaragua.

Talanga to Minas de Oro and Yoro – Given the choice the more interesting route to Minas de Oro goes from Comayagua (☞ see p.110). However if wanting to avoid the dirt roads and hills on that route, there is a newly paved road from Talanga that passes through pine forested hills to the old town of Cedras, and onto El Porvenir. At present it continues as a dirt road to Marale and Sulaco before joining up with a route from Minas de Oro to Yoro. In the next few years this road will be paved all the way to Yoro.

The junction for Esquias and Minas de Oro has a sign, and is on a flat straight stretch a few km before El Porvenir. This is a well compacted dirt road, with some eroded sections, passing a few villages with a couple of shops. The last few km over the hills to the junction for Minas de Oro, is particularly pretty. (☞ see p.112 for **Minas de Oro** and beyond).

El Porvenir is not the prettiest of towns to head for, although the climb shortly afterwards through the forested hills to Yoculecteca is beautiful. Onwards to Marale, the dusty wide road climbs through sparsely forested hills, with views toward the Montanas de La Flor.

Talanga to Limones, 120km – This main road is paved and in good condition, it's not that busy, but the traffic can be fast. There are some pretty pine forested hills to climb, otherwise it's fairly uninteresting with widespread agriculture and a couple of wood mills. Guimaca (55km) is 2km off the road to the right and has a hospedaje, follow the road all the way to the town plaza, it's pleasant place to stop for the night, and the way toward the El Chile reserve (see below). **Campamento** is another possibility, with some basic accommodation. **Limones** only has a few shops and comedors, and it's where the cross country route to La Union and Olanchito starts, see the next page.

If time is short it's worth taking a bus on this section and cycling onwards to La Union If heading toward Catacamas or Juticalpa it's worth considering taking a bus the whole way, and saving time for the more beautiful onward routes.

Guimaca to Teupasenti and onto Danli, 110km

126

NB Allow 2 days for this route. There is no accommodation, so camp discretely or with permission in a secure place. Its necessary to be able to ask directions regularly. There are only one or two shops for very basic supplies in the villages. Its not recommended after significant rain.
The ITMB map should not be relied upon for navigating on this route
From Guaimaca, the dirt road meanders through the pine forest, undulating heavily all the way. After about 20km the road divides:
To the right – leads to San Marcos, on the edge of the reserve. There are peace corps locally helping to develop the reserve, try to make contact from Guimaca for more information.
To the left – the road follows the valley through the spread out settlement of Rio Abajo and comes to another junction, (left leads toward to a village called El Chelon No1) turn right across the river, and start to climb around the other side of the valley, this dirt road meanders through the pine forest, passing isolated houses. At the next two junctions turn left, the road starts to climb steeply after the second junction, eventually emerging into a more open landscape, there are beautiful views westwards of the El Chile Reserve.

The first village come to is Santa Cruz(shop). Onwards there are several different roads, although the route regularly passes houses, keep asking for the way to San Isidro. The dirt road becomes a track in parts and would be difficult after rain, most of these highlands have been cleared for agriculture, which means excellent all round views. San Isidro is another small vilage, with a shop. Onwards the road descends, steeply and with loose stone in places, through the pine forest toward Teupasenti. This large village sits in a pretty valley and is the trading centre for a large area. There is a long climb out, into more agricultural highlands, before the road descends to Las Crucitas. It's then another 29km on the main road to Danli.

Limones–Olanchito

Limones to La Union (for La Muralla National Park), 60km – The main reason for taking this route is to visit the La Muralla national park, however the scenery is beautiful and the dirt roads are relatively quiet. It is the most peaceful and scenic way to the Caribbean coast.

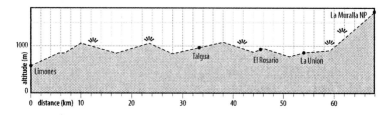

The wide dirt road is used by occasional logging traffic, and climbs over several beautiful pine forested hills and ridges, with mainly ranchland in the valleys between. There are a couple of smaller settlements nearer La Union with shops for basic food and water needs.

There are occasional buses from Juticalpa to La Union if wanting to save energy or time.

La Union

The town is quiet, has a large central square, a couple of basic accommodations, and several comedors. It's a good place to rest, before the climb up to the national park.

NB Apparently it is now mandatory to organise a guide with the Cohdefor office in La Union, before exploring the longer walking trails

La Union to La Muralla National park – The beginning of the 15km road is easy to find at the back left of the plaza. Be prepared as there are a couple of streams to ford in the first few km, you will get your feet wet! The dirt road then climbs steeply through the pine forest, further up are coffee plantations, more verdant vegetation, and isolated houses. Near the top, the park's visitors centre is to the right and just above the first and only obvious T-junction. To the left, the road levels out giving excellent views, after a couple of km it then starts to descend towards El Dictamo. This gives beautiful views of the park, there is a comedor in this village if required. The climb back is steep and stoney in places, onward routes have not been explored.

La Muralla National Park
There is still a substantial portion of intact forest in this park. Several trails lead from the visitors centre, although some are not particularly well maintained, so a guide is a good idea. The areas of cloud forest have a good biodiversity, and apparently a large quetzal population. There are areas of old logging, meaning some parts of the lower forest are still regrowing, this does allow for some good views.

The park visitors centre also has basic accommodation, but it is not always open, check with the office in La Union. Camping or hammock slinging in the grounds are a reasonable option, although it can get cool at night.

La Union to Saba-Olanchito highway about 80km
NB From La Union northwards, the road is remote, with only a couple of small settlements straggling the road. There were a spate of highway robberies a few years ago. Check locally on the current situation, this road is the most beautiful and peaceful way to ride toward the Caribbean coast, if unsure there is at least one bus a day.

The first part of this journey is predominatley through forest, the quiet road undulates, with some reasonable climbs out of a couple of valleys.

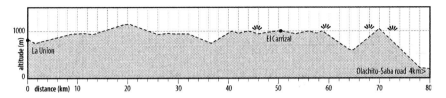

There is very little traffic on this dirt road. On the hill before Carrizal the scenery opens up and there are some amazing views of the distant mountains and deep valleys, although it's hotter with lack of shade. The road then climbs and descends some steeper mountain slopes, with more loose stone , there are excellent views for compensation.

The ITMB map is inaccurate between Carrizal and the main road

For last few km the stony road follows a river down to a junction on the Olanchito-Sava road:

To Saba, 42km – turn right, this straight, good quality, paved road descends gently, a nice change to the previous rough roads. The scenery is mainly dryland agriculture, with mountains to the south. **Sava** is a functional though uninteresting town, just off the main road. It has a few basic accommodations if needed.

To Olanchito, 13km – turn left, there is a gentle uphill on this fast road, the roadside scenery is mainly agricultural. Olanchito has a mix of accommodations.The town has good markets, a relaxed atmosphere and is rarely visited by tourists.

NB Given the choice Olanchito is the nicer place to spend a night

The routes over the mountains between Olanchito and La Ceiba, via Yaruca would be very hard this way round, as the gradients are so much steeper. There would be a lot of walking. Routes toward Yoro are unresearched, the roads are unpleasantly dusty, and have regular traffic. If they are paved in the future, this might be an interesting direction to explore.
☞ see p.121 for onward routes

Tegucigalpa–Nicaragua
Tegucicalpa to Yuscaran and Danli, 70km – From the Capital, follow the signs to Danli, and get ready for a climb out of the city basin, on a good paved road. Further up the mountain

sides are lined with pine trees, and there are one or two places to stop for food. At the top the views are beautiful, although its normally misty by the time it takes to get there. The descent into the agricultural valley of Zamorano is long and fast, this settlement has a couple of shops and comedors and is a pleasant place to stop for a break.

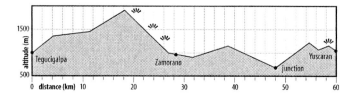

Climbing around the side of the valley to the Yuscaran turn-off is not hard but seems that way after such a long downhill and there is little shade. From the turning there's another 500m of climbing through the pine forest, including negotiating a valley higher up. The paved road is steep in places, but is wonderfully quiet.

Yuscaran
A beautiful, well preserved colonial mining town, with good views over the dry plains toward Nicaragua. There are a few places to stay, the nicest as usual, on the plaza.
The town has a reputation from producing good quality alcohol, called Guaro.
It's worth exploring the lush mountains behind the town. There are several, different steep paths for walking and a couple of winding tracks for off-roading.

Yuscaran to Oropoli, 20km – The dirt road goes from the top left (if looking up uphill) of the plaza and is a fun descent through changing vegetation, with rapidly increasing temperatures. The dry land trees and scrub further down contrasting starkly with the lush vegetation around Yuscaran. As the road starts to level out in the arid plains, agriculture dominates. There are no places for water or supplies until Oropoli, so take enough supplies. This dusty large village has a few shops and a plaza. Check in Yuscaran before leaving for the bus times to get back from Oropoli, there are only occasional pick-ups.

129

Further adventures
The ITMB map should not be relied upon for navigation in these areas.
For cyclists wanting a challenge, there is an interesting route from Oropoli to the pretty town of **San Antonio de Flores**. The tracks are extremely rough, slow and very beautiful. Ask for

directions locally.

The route crosses the river at the back of Oropoli, bear left at the first junction, then after another 3-4km bear right, ask directions if unsure at any stage. This track climbs around a headland then descends into a valley, the river will need to be forded, although there may now be a bridge. The climb up the other side is hard work with much loose stone, but rewarded at the top with good views. After a bumpy, level section the track climbs up to a more substantial dirt road, take a left, there are good views, before the road descends to San Antonio.

From this village there are one or two morning buses back to Tegucigalpa, via Guinope and Zamorano, this route takes longer than it looks, winding around the pine clad mountainsides and through a couple of deep valleys *or* unresearched routes descend to the Pacific coast.
NB This is one of the poorest parts of Honduras.

Yuscaran to Danli, 70km – After returning to the main road, the route is straightforward, there are two climbs, with pine forest on the hills giving some shade, in the valleys, the land has been cultivated. There are a few settlements and roadside comedors, but the gaps between them can be long, so it's worth taking enough water and food.
NB Some of the buses on this route have luggage compartments that are too small for a bike, but they will, if possible, squeeze it in somewhere.

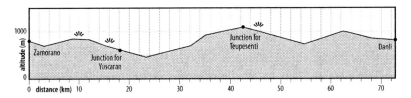

For an off-road alternative there is an unreseached dirt road from near Oropoli, along the dusty valley bottom, it cuts through to San Matais near Danli, ask locally for advice in Yuscaran.

Danli

This agricultural town is a nice place to relax, without having any particular attractions. The markets at the back of town are busy and the people laid back and friendly. The locally produced cigars are an important business and good quality. If needing to overnight, there is a variety of accommodation.

Danli to Nicaraguan frontier, 27km – There's a gentle downhill nearly all the way to the town

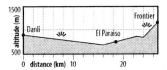

of El Paraiso, another friendly place and a couple of km off the main road. It is hot and there isn't much shade so this would be a journey to avoid in the midday.

Onwards there's an undulating climb, with a steep last couple of km to the frontier.

Formalities are straightforward at this busy border. There is a departure tax of a few dollars from Honduras and a slightly higher entrance tax for Nicaragua, there are big signs against corruption to put your mind at rest!
NB This is one border where you may need some form of paperwork for your bike, a receipt or something similar with the frame number on it should suffice.

Nicaragua

NB This section just gives a taste of the country, and will be added to with the rest of central America in future publications.

The northern third of Nicaragua is covered on the Honduras ITMB map.

Nicaragua is becoming found as a place to enjoy, not just pass through on the way to Costa Rica, it's culturally very much alive, and with incredible volcanoes and lakes. In terms of cycling it is perhaps more limited, but there are some fantastic routes in the north of the country, further south most of the country is low lying hot plains, which might be easier than hills, but the temperatures will make it worth avoiding in the midday hours.

Entry and tourist taxes are above board, though they are relatively steep. A bicycle may well need some form of receipt, and the ensuing paperwork will need to be presented on departure. Avoid the money changers, it's a short hop downhill to the banks in Ocotal.

Frontier to Ocotal, 22km – A great introduction to Nicaragua as it almost entirely downhill, the good quality paved road passes a few isolated communities and follows a pretty valley down to Ocotal.

Ocotal – A pleasant colonial town, with banks to change money in and plenty of shops for supplies. The town centre is a few blocks east of the main highway.

Ocotal to Esteli, 65km – A pleasant ride through mainly dry landscapes, the roads are good quality, although get much busier after the junction with the Somoto road. Condega is nice place to spend the night and famous for it's local pottery. There are several hills on this road and the climb up from Condega to Esteli would be taxing.

Esteli

This is an excellent base for exploring the surrounding mountains and nature reserves. The town suffered greatly during the civil war, leaving a few bullet hole reminders, it is now mostly a modern busy settlement. The centre is to the west of the main highway. There are several cafes and food stalls around the main square, along with banks, shops and internet etc.

SIDE TRIPS

There is a track to waterfalls and a lovely ridge of forested hills that starts close to the hospital, south of town.

If wanting a real adventure continue on this road until it joins with another wider dirt road to San Nicholas, from where there are rough roads all the way to Santa Rosa del Perion (accommodation). This is a journey not take lightly, it will take several hours and need some Spanish to ask directions regularly.

Towards the Pacific coast are hot straight roads, the views when crossing the line of volcanoes are pretty, but for the most part they would be uninteresting.

Miraflores nature reserve – There are detailed large-scale maps of this reserve available from a tourist office, 2 blocks east of the main square. There are many excellent trails and dirt roads, which lead toward La Concordia and San Rafael del Norte, where there is a basic, but pleasant hospedaje. Onwards is a good paved road to Jinoteca, again with basic accommodation.

131

Jinoteca to Matagalpa, 30km – This is one of the most beautiful bike rides in Nicaragua, although not without some strenuous climbing. There are patches of rain forest left on top of the mountains and in between is pretty, highland pasture and vegetable farms, some of the produce is sold on the roadside. Fabulous views westwards can be seen from the road around Arenal (shops). After a long descent, Matagalpa has a few places to stay and is an interesting town.

Leon and the Pacific coast
As with the rest of this region the western plains are very hot, if cycling, starting early and having a long siesta are important. A bike is very useful for getting around the city, and there are several dirt tracks among the small hills around Leon, for some off-road fun.

Granada and surrounds
Masaya and the nearby volcanic park is worth a visit if passing by on the road from Managua. There are some gorgeous tracks around the lake near Granada, and cycling up to the Vol. Mombacho is an excellent hard ride along forest-shaded roads.
    Onwards from Granada are boats to Isla de Ometepe which is highly recommended by all who visit.

Notes

- El Salvador was avoided on good advice, as the roads are much busier, the Pacific coast is very hot and crime can be a big problem.
- Things are changing rapidly in Central America, meaning any guide can quickly become dated. What is for sure is there will be increasing numbers of cars and the roads will gradually be improved. Please notify the author at **cyclecentralamerica@btopenworld.com** of new routes and any invalid or changing information. The guide will be updated for future editions and the sources will be gratefully acknowleged.
- Of the routes researched, all have been travelled (some several times) by the author and 95% have actually been cycled.
- The cross sections are good representations of the topography to be encountered, they are not perfect, and don't include every bump. Dotted lines signify dirt roads, a solid line, those that are paved.
- The maps are hand drawn and include all new roads, although aren't exactly to scale.
- Apologies for the lack of correct punctuation for the Spanish names.
- The general assumption for route descriptions was that nearly all cyclists want to travel from north to south through this region. Because of the framework of researched routes, this means that occasionally it may be necessary to follow a route described in reverse, any feedback on this would be gratefully received.

Abbrieviations included within the text:

Km or km	Kilometre
NP	National park
Vol.	Volcano
M or m	Metres
Sto/Sta	Santo/santa(saint)

The following conversions change imperial to metric measurements

1000 feet is about 305 metres	1 kilometre is about 0.6 miles
1000 metres (1km) is about 3280 feet	1 mile is about 1.6 kilometres

Volunteer work
If wanting to volunteer on a bicycle related project:

- **Fidesma** take bikes from **Pedals for Progress** and are based in San Andreas Ixtapa (Guatemala), selling them on to those who couldn't normally afford one. Contact will only be possible locally and some Spanish is needed. For basic background information check the **www.P4p.Org** website.
- **Mayapedal** take bikes from **Bikes not Bombs** and other groups, and sell on some of the them, turning the others into well pumps, corn grinders, trailers and other very useful devices for the rural poor. They are now based in Antigua in Guatemala, and contact can be made through **www.Pedalpower.Org** (Pto for some photos from this project)
- **CESTA** based in San Salvador, are a very professional charitable outfit, taking several thousand bikes a year, and they do occasionally take on volunteers, check the Net for how to make contact.

Some of the varied examples of bicycle
recycling at the Mayapedal project, Guatemala

Basic Spanish

Learning to converse in Spanish, will enhance your experience massively, just making an effort, will often bring smiles.

A pocket dictionary is essential to help gain a vocabularly.

The following phrases will help to get around most every day situations

PLEASANTRIES/GREETINGS/GENERAL CONVERSATION

Hello	Hola	Cheers	Salud
Good day	Buenas Dias/	I'm going	Me voy
Good afternoon/night	Buenas Tardes/Noches	Perhaps	Tal vez
Goodbye	Adios	What's going on?	Que pasa?
See you tomorrow/later	Hasta Manana/ Luego	You don't say	No diga
How are you?	Como esta/ estas?	Never mind	No importa
Fine thankyou	Muy bien gracias	Take care	Cuidado
How do you say	Como se dice	Excuse me	Con permiso
What is your name?	Como se llama?	You don't say	No diga
My name is	Me llamo	What a pity	Que lastima
Thankyou	Gracias	Yes/no	Si/No
I don't understand	No entiendo/comprendo	Please	Por favor
Leave me alone	Dejame solo	Go away	Vayase
Where do you come from?	De donde eres?	Which part?	Que Parte?
I'm coming	Ya voy	To cheer up	Dar animo
To be exhausted	No poder mas	To be broke	Estar roto
Too late	Ya es tarde	Ready to go	Listo

DIRECTIONS AND ROUTE DESCRIPTIONS

Can you draw a map please	Puede dibuje un mapa, por favor		
Which way....?	Que via/Cual direccion?	One way	Una via
How many Km is....?	Quantos kilometres es....?	Steep	Empinado
Where is...	Donde es...	North	Norte
To the right/left	A la derecha/Izquierda	South	Sur
The next	La Proxima	East	Est
Straight	Derecho, recto	West	Oeste
Crossroads/Junction	Cruce (de caminos)/Desvio	Less	Menos
Flat	Plano	More	Mas
The top	La Encima	Slow	Despacio
Private	Privado	Fast	Rapido
Salida	Way out	Open	Abierto
Give way	Ceda el Paso	Closed	Cerrado
Danger	Peligro	Big road	Carretera
Climb (Road)	Subida/Cuesta	Footpath	Sendero
City/Town square	Zocalo/ plaza	Track	Piste
Street	Avenida/ Calle	Small road	Camino
Near	cerca	Far	Lejo

ACCOMMODATION

Cheap hotel	Hospedaje, Hostal or Pension
Youth hostel	Auberge de Jovenes
Hotel	Hotel
Where is the nearest cheap hotel?	Donde esta mas cerca hospedaje?
Is there a cheaper place/room?	Hay un lugar/cuarto mas barato?
Can I camp here?	Puedo encamapa aqui?
Can I rent a room for the night?	Puedo renta un cuarto para la noche?
Is there a hot shower?	Hay una ducha caliente?
Is there a fan?	Hay una ventilador?
Hotel/ Hostel	Hopedajae/Hostel/Pension/Hotel/Posada
Are there any rooms for tonight?	Hay cuartos para esta noche?
Have you single/double rooms?	Tiene cuartos single/doble?
Can I see it/them?	Puedo verlo/s ?
Toilets/bathroom	Servicios/Banos
Private/communal bathroom	Banos privado/communal
Rooms	Cuartos/habitaciones
Bed (s)	Cama (s)

BIKE PARTS

Bicycle	Bicycleta	Saddle	Asiento
Chain	Cadena	Headset	Copas
Pedal	Pedal	Cable	Cable
Rear derrailer	Carisso	Tyre	Llantra
Front derrrailer	Decorrilador	Wheel	Rueda
Bottom bracket	Caja central	Rim	Aro
Axle	Eje	Brake pads	Gomas
Bearings	Bolas	Bike rack	Parilla
Brakes	Frenos	Patches	Patches
Inner tube	Tubo	Glue	Goma

136

BUYING THINGS

How much is....this/ that?	Cuanto es.......esto/eso?
How much does it cost?	Cuanto cuesto/vale?
Can I have....	Puedo tener....
Food/Meal	Comida
Pure water	Agua pura
End transaction/OK	Cheque, Igual
(Small) Change	Sencillo, pisto, suelto
Small shops	Pulperias (Honduras), Tiendas, Tendejones (Mexico)
Petrol/ Gas station	Gasolineria
Market	Mercado
Eating house	Loncherias
Place for cooked snacks	Golosinas
House where food can be bought	Cassita
What do you have to eat	Que tiene para comer
I don't eat meat	No como carne

NUMBERS

One	Uno	Twenty	Viente
Two	Dos	Thirty	Treinte
Three	Tres	Forty	Cuarenta
Four	Cuarto	Fifty	Cincuenta
Five	Cinco	Sixty	Sesenta
Six	Seis	Seventy	Setenta
Seven	Siete	Eighty	Ochenta
Eight	Ocho	Ninety	Noventa
Nine	Nueve	Hundred	Cien
Ten	Diez	Thousand	Mil

DAYS

Monday	Lunes	Tuesday	Martes
Wednesday	Miercoles	Thursday	Jueves
Friday	Viernes	Saturday	Sabado
Sunday	Domingo		

MONTHS

January	Enero	July	Julio
February	Febrero	August	Agosto
March	Marzo	September	Septiembre
April	Abril	October	Octubre
May	Mayo	November	Noviembre
June	Junio	December	Deciembre

TIME

What time is it?	Que hora es?	Twenty to four	Quatro menos veinte
How many hours to...	Quantos horas a...	One thirty	Una y Media
Seven fourteen	Siete catorce	Six O'clock	La Seis (en punto)

137

PLACES

Palacio municipal	Local government offices		
Post office	El correo		
Police (station)	Policia (comisaria de policia)		
Hot springs/ baths	Fuentes/ balnearios thermales		
Bus station	La terminal (estacion) de autobuses		
Basic restaurant	Comedor	Lookout	Mirador
Mountain range	Cordiller	Mountains	Sierra
Beach	Playa	Point, headland	Punta (Pta)
Bridge	Puente	Farm	Finca/granja
Plain, savannah	Llano	Bay	Bahia
Cave, cavern	Cueva, Gruta	Jungle	Selva
Forest	Bosque	Supermarket	Supermercado

MEDICAL WORDS

Pain	Dolor	Head	Cabeza
Wound	**La Herida**	**Bone**	**Hueso**
Cut	El Corte	Arm	Brazo
Bruise	**Contusion**	**Wrist**	**Munecas**
Foot	El pie	Muscles	Musculos
Leg	**La pierna**	**Knee**	**Rodilla**
Health centre	Centro de Salud	Doctor	Medica

WEATHER

It's cold/hot/warm/cool	**Hace frio/caliente/calor/fresco**
Misty	Neblima
Wind	**Viento**
Sun	Sol
Damp or wet	**Humedad**
Rain	Lluvia
Cloudy	**Nubioso**
Clouds	Nubes
Dry	**Seco**

BASIC VERBS

To want	**Quierer**	**To go**	**Ir**
I want	Quiero	I go	Voy
You want (familiar)	**Quieres**	**You go**	**Vas**
You want (formal)	Quiere	You go	Va
He/ she/ it wants	**Quiere**	**He/she /it goes**	**Va**
We want	Queremos	We go	Vamos
They want	**Quieren**	**They go**	**Van**

To Be	**Ser (Permanent form)**	**Estar (Temporary form)**
I am	Soy	Estoy
You are (familiar)	**Eres**	**Estas**
You are (formal)	Es	Esta
He/She/ it is	**Es**	**Esta**
We are	Somos	Estamos
They are	**Son**	**Estan**

To Have	**Tener**	**To be able**	**Pueder**
I have	Tengo	I Can	Puedo
You have (fam)	**Tienes**	**You can**	**Puedes**
You have (for)	Tiene	You can	Puede
He/she/it has	**Tiene**	**He/she/it can**	**Puede**
We have	Tenemos	We can	Puedemos
They have	**Tienen**	**They can**	**Pueden**

138

Latin words

Cenotes are pools of fresh water of varying size, in the limestone plateau. Some are underground.

Cabanas are palm thatch huts of various sizes, used on beaches everywhere

Mestizos are people of mixed race, latin and indigenous, evolved into the name Mexico

Gringo (Green go), originally the local name for US soldiers, now used widely for all foreigners

Milpa is a small field of maize and/or beans

Aldeas are small villages

Plaza or sometimes parque central, describes the main square in villages and towns

Zocalo is the main square in a city

Stelae are the carved monoliths in and around Mayan ruins

Latinization of Spanish

It's common for ITO or ITA to be added after normal Spanish words, it lessens the original meaning, and needs a more laid back interpretation

E.gs

Ahorita means in a bit

Ahora means now

Easy mistranslations

Many Spanish words look similar to english words, here are a couple of the awkward examples that have very different meanings.

Embarazada	means	Pregnant
Ropa		Clothes
Exito		Success

139

140

141

143